Start It, Sell It and Make a Mint

Start It, Sell It and Make a Mint

20 Wealth-Creating Secrets for Business Owners

Joe John Duran, CFA

WILEY

John Wiley & Sons, Inc.

For Jennifer, my wonderful wife, who always sees the best in me, and for our precious daughters, Charlotte and Juliette. I love you.

ISBN: 0-471-47961-6

Printed in the United States of America

10 9 8 7 6 5 4 3 2 1

Contents

Introduction

Wow! What a feeling. It's December 17, 2001. New York is in full holiday spirit, glistening with Christmas lights and still bustling with holiday shoppers late at night. The three of us are sitting in the lounge of a luxurious hotel; cold drinks on the table, with smiles on our faces, and each of us with millions of dollars to show for 10 years of exhilarating work.

After years of building, after a couple of near misses, after months of review and excruciating negotiations with a company many, many times our size, after pages and pages of paperwork, even after the paralysis we all felt in the midst of the September 11 tragedy, we successfully sold our baby, Centurion Capital, to GE Financial, the financial subsidiary of one of the world's largest and best-run companies—General Electric.

As we look back at that particular moment, the only thing we all agree on is how blessed we feel. We realize now how little we knew when we started, and how lucky we are that the many things we learned over that 10-year period did not destroy the company while we were learning. How fortunate we are to live in a country like America, where good fortune can smile upon anyone in such a spectacular way.

The genesis for this book occurred at that moment. I wanted to share with all of my enterprising friends the 20 vital secrets that I've learned from the process of growing a thriving and valuable business—the vital truths they need to know to help them to build their piece of the great American Dream and, just as importantly, how to attain the highest possible value for their business when it's time to sell.

Throughout the expansion of our company, whenever I looked in the bookstore for guidance all I found were books on how large public companies succeeded. But that advice was seldom applicable to my independent business and the unique challenges that we faced because of our size and the fact that we were an owner-run company. So, with the help of many friends and business colleagues, we created a book that speaks directly to the independent business owner, regardless of industry or size. Whether you have a small pet shop in Boston, Massachusetts, a chain of real estate agencies in Los Angeles, California, or anything in between, this book will offer you valuable strategies. We entrepreneurs all face similar challenges as we grow our businesses and take risks that many dare not take. This book seeks to address the most common issues.

The Dream of Freedom

The Dream
You wake up every morning knowing that your day's work will be set by you, for the benefit of those you choose, in an environment that is rewarding both financially and emotionally. Your clients love you, your employees are happy, and you are answerable to only yourself. You are happy and free from worries.

The Reality
Setting the rules, controlling your future and building a legacy are all exciting prospects, and yet very few people successfully reach this dream. In fact, many people end up broken hearted and in financial distress, or disappointed to find that they have basically created a job for themselves—they are incapable of taking vacations and they have no idea how to create an exit strategy. Many end up frustrated at how hard they work for a modest income pay off.

Consider these extraordinary small-business statistics from the Small Business Administration: More than 22 million small businesses already exist in America. They account for 99 percent of all American businesses. They employ 53 percent of the private work force and contribute over half of the nation's private gross domestic product. Yet, out of one million businesses that start up each year, *one-half fail within the first two years* because of a lack of financing, management discipline, or basic entrepreneurial skills. Of the privately owned businesses, over two million of them will experience a change in ownership every year, with little experience by the seller in how to make a healthy transition.

However, it doesn't have to be that way. You can take steps to make the reality a lot more similar to the dream. Our goal in writing this book is to:

- Share key insights that will help the entrepreneur build a thriving business that is fulfilling, rewarding and exciting. To build a business that gives them freedom.

- Provide a step-by-step guide to the practical implementation of the secrets to give the entrepreneur and prospective entrepreneur immediate benefit.

- Teach the business owner how to avoid the costly mistakes that leave so many individual business owners disillusioned, disheartened, and in financial difficulty.

- Show the business owner how to build a valuable enterprise that can be sold at a premium.

Over the years, I saw many of our competitors fall by the wayside, and I helped several smaller firms to become more successful. I found common traits among the failures as well as among the successes. By showing you how companies have succeeded by doing business the right way, I believe this book will improve the likelihood of prosperity for any business. Besides giving the entrepreneur a competitive edge, the people-oriented principles can help make the management of a business more fun for owners, managers, and associates alike.

I have included excerpts from interviews conducted with dozens of business owners in a myriad of industries, all of whom provide great real-life examples of these secrets at work in the real world. I think you will find their stories to be alternately funny, scary, and exciting, but most of all, they will help you to see how each of these secrets applies to the real world.

Our company managed money for many thousands of investors, and yet I noticed that those with real self-made wealth (more than five million dollars in liquid assets) were without exception owners of businesses to which they had contributed for a significant period of time. An overwhelming majority of them were self-employed, or started with a small company near its inception, and then sold it or created a capitalization event. Every one of these people said they had been incredibly "lucky." But after we spoke, it became obvious that they had created their luck by doing all the right things.

What Are These 20 Vital Secrets?

Each secret represents a vital truth associated with owning and operating a business successfully. These are the business truths every entrepreneur wishes he had known at the outset of his business rather than having to painfully learn them on the job. While some folks might simply be lucky, it is more likely that those who managed to succeed, knowingly or unknowingly, learned many of these fundamental business truths the hard way.

The secrets are divided into two categories: those for building a company, and those for selling a company. There are secrets for each segment of your business, from sales to finance.

As is true for most things in this world, there will be exceptions to these secrets. In other words, some people succeeded while not implementing these secrets in their entirety but excelling in one or several of the other secrets. It is, in fact, unusual to find a company that applies all of these rules all of the time. However they do represent the ideals that every business can strive for.

How Should You Use This Book?

You will notice that every section begins with a tale, or parable, illustrating a moral that is emphasized throughout the chapter. These tales share insights in a fun way. Some were shared with me, and some were invented; however, all are African in nature, primarily to pay homage to the continent on which I grew up.

For each secret the book provides real-life experiences—my own and those of other businesspeople representing a wide array of industries— as a way of illustrating how the rules function in the real world. Each chapter provides insight into what this rule should mean to you and then guides you step-by-step on applying and making this rule work in your business immediately.

Each chapter is written as a stand-alone section. You do not have to read it all in sequence but some of the secrets do build on previous insights. Read the book initially from cover to cover. Then go to the area of your business that you feel requires the most attention and try to implement the steps we've outlined. There are far too many strategies here to do all of them immediately. Alternately, you can simply go to the subject that you want to focus on and apply the lessons to that particular part of your business. We have also built an interactive report card online that you can access at www.startitsellit.com. This report card along with several other tools on the site are there to help your company.

Get Ready, Get Set, Go!

I hope you will find this book a valuable companion as you grow your business. As part of a commitment I made when I was 14 years old in Africa, half of all net proceeds from the sale of this book are donated toward teaching entrepreneurship to underprivileged children and toward helping people develop small businesses in disadvantaged regions. Therefore your purchase will help someone else in some small way. Congratulations for having the courage to shape your own future. Thank you for doing all the things that make America unique, and may you be immensely "lucky"!

Chapter ONE

My Story

How we grew our company, what we experienced at the different stages

of growth, and why following the rules we learned is so important.

Shake It Off

The Tale of the Persistent Donkey

There was once an old farmer walking his faithful donkey through the dusty fields of Africa. The summer had been particularly dry, and he was going to see how the heat had affected the out-reaches of his farm. Soon the farmer came to his favorite sitting spot, an old well where he used to get his water. Needing a rest, he stopped and looked down the dry well.

His donkey also looked, because he too was thirsty. But unfortunately, the frail old donkey lost his footing and fell down the well. Watching the accident, the farmer saw that the donkey was fine, but that he was trapped.

After a few minutes of thought, the farmer sadly realized that he had no other choice but to bury his old friend. So taking a shovel, the farmer started throwing sand down the well, all the while apologizing to the donkey.

"I'm sorry, old friend," said the farmer, "but this is all I can do."

For hours, the farmer shoveled and tossed sand into the well, working desperately to keep the donkey's suffering to a minimum. As he realized that he must be getting close to filling the well, the farmer caught his breath and turned around to see his progress.

As he did, the donkey's head popped out of the well. Before the farmer was able to speak, the donkey jumped out of the well and ran off. Watching his old friend, the farmer realized that the donkey had been shaking off the sand and stepping on it to rise to the top of the well.

The moral of the story: The world will continue to heap dust on you, but if you can shake it off and keep stepping, you'll eventually see daylight.

■■■■

At the end of May 2002, I formally left the company I'd helped to create. I had started my voyage 10 years earlier, and during that time our small group had managed to create what so many Americans dream of—real wealth. My partners and I had taken a small investment firm, and through countless challenges and opportunities, built it into a company that was being bought by General Electrics GE Financial for millions of dollars. I had reached a goal set 20 years before in Africa.

In 1982, after a particularly inspiring episode of *Dallas,* I turned to my mother and said, "I'm going to make my fortune in America." There were a few obstacles in front of me however—I was 14, a mediocre student of no particular talent, and I happened to be in Harare, Zimbabwe.

It's still almost impossible for me to imagine that I went from being a 14 year old watching fuzzy images on TV in Zimbabwe to a 34-year-old multi-millionaire living in the United States. How in the world could it have worked out so well?

I grew up in Zimbabwe, a beautiful but challenging country in Southern Africa. Like most of Africa, Zimbabwe was always in some state of turmoil, whether it was a civil war, government unrest, a drought, or a new financial crisis. My mother and step-dad were entrepreneurs, and for much of my young life, they suffered through financial stress before becoming successful. They worked long and hard, but we always had dinner together and they often talked about the latest challenges in their businesses. Growing up in Africa teaches you how to live with constant risk and uncertainty—not bad training when you plan to run a company!

Like many of the entrepreneurs I interviewed for this book, I was a modest student with lots of Bs and Cs and "could try harder" or "is often distracted" comments on my report card. I played a lot of sports and hung around with my friends. Besides being a little more outgoing than most, I was quite average in most areas.

After high school, I set off for Europe to travel the world before deciding what I should do next. Unfortunately, two weeks into my "world tour" I was mugged by a couple of thugs in London. They took my backpack and money belt. I was 18; I had no clothes, no money, and no passport. I was stuck in my first snowfall in a foreign country. I walked around in the gloomy London winter and thought about calling my parents for help. I knew that they would have wanted me to call, but not only was I embarrassed, I wanted to prove to them that I could make it on my own. So instead I focused on how I was going to get by. I guess that's the kind of decision you can make when you're 18. I'm not sure that I'd be as stubborn today, but I'm so happy that I didn't call them. That decision changed the rest of my life. I slept in the South Kensington train station that night, and the next day I found a job as a night watchman at a youth hostel.

From there I spent a year traveling, running with the bulls in Pamplona, and drinking beer in Munich during Oktoberfest. While traveling, I picked up odd jobs wherever I could, doing things such as picking weeds in Holland, serving drinks in Denmark, and checking people into a youth hostel in Portugal. Hardly the world's most glamorous jobs, but I always worked with fun people. I never worried about getting by again because whenever I would run low on money, I'd find a job doing something along the way. It could never be as bleak as it was that night in London.

Eventually, I came to the United States and studied finance and marketing at a college in the Midwest. After graduating, I moved to Los Angeles to be with my future wife Jennifer, and searched high and low for a job in the financial services industry. Soon I found an opportunity with a small company that paid little money, but offered me the potential of making it in the future. Ten years had passed since I'd told my mother my intentions, and I was now starting to chase the American dream.

In 1992, I joined FundMinder, a small investment firm that had just been incorporated. The two guys who were starting it needed some inexpensive help. The firm charged a quarterly fee for its services, was generating a little over one million dollars in revenue, and had fewer than five employees when I joined the company. At this point, it was not a viable business. Unlike many investment advisors at the time, who pursued large investors, our clients were mostly retirees who had somewhere between $10,000 and $50,000 to invest and couldn't afford to take big risks with their money. Because of this, we would try to safely grow their accounts by investing conservatively.

In joining, I became part of a small team that included Dr. Bob, an ivy league-educated PhD, and Werner, an experienced resesarch analyst. Bob was the long-term thinker and constant worrier of the group, a very intelligent, articulate, and opinionated man. Werner was the detail-oriented technician, experienced, humble and immensely likable. I was the optimistic operator and marketer for the business, outspoken and perhaps a little overconfident. Of the three of us, only Bob had experienced significant business success in the past. At 24, I was quite a bit younger than my partners, who were in their early fifties, but we shared common values and a vision of what we wanted to accomplish.

In the beginning, we all had different aspirations. Not thinking ahead, we simply concentrated on building a business that paid everyone well and that we enjoyed working in. During the course of our 10-year journey, Werner decided to retire, and Bob and I worked to grow the company until it was sold.

Over the next 10 years, we grew from a few hundred small clients to many thousands of large clients. The company also ballooned from much less than one hundred million dollars under management to well over two billion dollars, and our annual revenues increased from about one million dollars to many tens of millions of dollars by the time we sold. We changed our name to Centurion Capital to reflect our growing status as a nationally known and respected investment firm.

As you're probably aware, running your own business is both exhilarating and unbelievably nerve racking. Your work is not simply a job, but a piece of you. Having a business is like raising a child—according to every business owner interviewed for this book. It's emotional, difficult, and draining, and yet incredibly rewarding on many levels. And although you might think that no one can take care of or understand your baby as well as you, your business will grow, change, and ultimately become completely self-reliant if you allow it to.

Throughout my years with the business, there were countless sleepless nights, innumerable highs, moments of anguish and great pride, and one final good-bye. But rather than get ahead of myself, let's first talk about what my partners and I went through to grow our business into a thriving and valuable company.

■ ■ ■ ■

Once you get to a destination, it's easy to look back and distinguish the important decisions from the trivial ones. It's also easy to recall when you were at a crossroads, even though it might not have seemed like it at the time. For us, as with most businesses, there were four distinct stages of growth and evolution:

1. The infant/toddler, or start-up stage (1992-1994).
2. The elementary child, or early growth stage (1994-1998).
3. The adolescent, or mature growth stage (1998-2000).
4. The adult, or the viable business stage (2000-2001).

To better explain these stages, I've compared them to the stages of human development. But before we begin, it is important to point out a major difference between businesses and people. Unlike people, many businesses will not grow or develop without a lot of prodding and pushing along the way. And as an entrepreneur, you need to push and prod your business until it reaches the point where it will grow by itself. This is the heart of what you are striving to accomplish.

Not surprisingly, many companies stay at a particular stage for a very long time. This often happens because the current situation is rewarding and fun for the business owner, and so growth and evolution stop. However, sometimes businesses stop growing because they've hit a growth ceiling. A growth ceiling is a point in a business's development when something significant needs to change in order for the company to keep growing. The more developed your business becomes, the more valuable it will be to someone else. What follows are the phases of our company's growth.

■■■■

1. The Infant, or Start-up Stage

"Well, folks, I want to thank you for coming this morning. I appreciate your attention and I hope we can work together in the future." It was a Saturday morning in 1994, and I was just wrapping up another seminar far from home. It was becoming easier to give presentations, and I'd conducted more seminars than I could count during the first two years with the company. Through trial and error, I'd found a niche speaking to people about protecting their investments. This particular seminar was for an extremely successful financial planner I'd been courting for months and who was working with me for the first time.

"That'll be $1,700," the planner said nonchalantly as he handed me the bill. I was genuinely shocked.

"Excuse me? You only had eight people at the seminar."

"Well, it cost a little more than expected to put this together," the planner smiled. Apparently, he was accustomed to receiving significant amounts of money as marketing support, but there was no way we could afford to pay that much for an eight-person seminar.

These are the kinds of things my partners and I had to get used to. In every industry there is a tug of war for clients, and whoever has them can command a premium. In this case, I only paid for breakfast, which was $250 including tip, and flew back home to my wife. Needless to say, the planner wasn't happy and never worked with us again.

■■■■

The birth of a business starts with an idea, and is followed by the actual formation of the company. Typically, people who create businesses have a passion for that particular industry, such as a dressmaker who starts a dress-manufacturing company, a cook who builds a restaurant, or a mechanic who creates his own auto repair company. In our case the original founder of FundMinder was Werner, a talented investment professional who loved managing money. In creating a new business, the transition from dream to reality was initially a humbling experience.

The Driving Force of an "Infant" or Start-up Business

As with a newborn or toddler, the driving force behind a newly formed business is survival. Just as a baby needs nourishment, attention, and support, a newly formed company needs cash and clients to nourish and support it.

What drives someone to start a business? Most often, the owner wants to control his future, as well as the benefits and rewards of his work. In short, these people are seeking to determine their own destiny, which is the heart of the American dream.

For myself, those first few years as an entrepreneur were fantastic but nerve racking. At FundMinder, everyone did everything because the roles and responsibilities were in constant flux. Incoming work simply went to the person who could do it. We conducted seminars, made calls, and even designed all the marketing materials. It has been said that an effective business leader must walk in the shoes of all of his employees. This means not only knowing what they do, but also being able to gauge how well they do it. I couldn't agree more.

The hard work began to pay off and our business soon took hold. In the beginning, we had no clear goals for the future, nor did we have a three-year business plan. Instead, those first few years revolved around two things: sales and product. Our focus was to create something valuable by spending all our time getting clients and trying to make enough money to pay the bills.

One of the downsides to creating your own work environment is the worry of paying all the invoices that come your way. Invoices can quickly become greater than you expect and at the same time, it takes longer for people to become clients than you planned. I heard similar stories from many entrepreneurs, and this was certainly true for us.

We had very little money in the bank; no one would lend us any because FundMinder didn't have any hard assets to borrow against. None of us were making much money, and we were trying to make each dollar go as far as possible. We barely made payroll every two weeks, and when traveling, I'd stay in cheap motels and take flights with lots of layovers to save money. We printed our marketing materials in black and white using our only printer. Any expense that required a couple thousand dollars was cause for serious discussion and consideration. Even when purchases were approved, we didn't spend any money unless enough cash was in the bank; we couldn't afford to spend future earnings. Had we not been so frugal, I'm not sure we could have stayed open for business in our initial stages.

Why Many Independent Businesses Don't Leave This Stage

Half of the businesses that start every year in the United States fail within their first two years, and there are two key reasons: first, there is insufficient cash to survive the wait and second, the owners treat the business as a hobby rather than a business.

We will discuss both of these in depth later in the book, but in our particular business, the challenge was cash management. Fortunately, we were careful with our expenses, and our revenue eventually increased to an amount that covered our fixed expenses. FundMinder spent a couple of years at this stage before moving to the next level, the elementary child or early growth stage.

■■■■

2. The Elementary Child, or Early Growth Stage

"Listen, Don, I know it's taking a little while but please hang in there. I promise it'll be worth it."

For the past several months, I'd been developing a wholesaler contract in order to recruit a great veteran salesman from one of our competitors. We couldn't afford to pay him a comparable salary, but we knew that if this worked out for him, we could hire others like him.

Don was tenacious, demanding, and tough, but I believed he was the catalyst that would elevate our company to the next level, so we came up with a unique contract to entice him. It would give him an ongoing revenue stream on any business he brought us. In essence, it would create security for his future. Very few firms in the industry were doing this for their wholesalers at the time, and it made our company distinctly attractive to him.

Once the contract was complete, he joined us and immediately became our toughest critic. Although Don was almost always right, his constant arguments drove me, as well as my managers, crazy. Don was also responsible for my first stress attack.

One Friday afternoon, he called and began ripping into me for a barrage of things we hadn't done in accordance with his liking. According to Don, he was about to starve, had been away from his home and family for a week, and was driving all across Texas in the rain just for us. All this, while I was supposedly enjoying the California sun from my comfy chair and living in the lap of luxury. (If you've worked with salesmen, you know they can have a flair for the dramatic at certain times.) Don continued his tirade, refusing to back down until he got the reaction he wanted. I was incredibly frustrated with the conversation because he refused to hear anything I was saying, and I soon noticed that it was getting much harder to breathe. My chest began to hurt, and I hung up on him because I was certain I was having a heart attack. At the time, I was 28.

This situation taught me a lot, and Don became both our top salesman and a good friend. He was one of the people I could always go to for an unfiltered opinion about the company. As I anticipated, he was also the building block upon which our company hired many outstanding people. In fact, he was so tough that the others we added were easy in comparison. Anyone who thinks being in sales is a tough job should try to run a sales force. Yet without a sales team it is next to impossible for any company to grow consistently.

■■■■

There are two ways to tell if a company has begun evolving into the early growth stage. First, departments begin to develop, and second, a sales force is created.

As the development of departments begins, distinct areas such as operations and sales are created, meaning that the decision-making process begins to include more people. As this happens, the owner is typically involved in important decisions, while smaller, detailed decisions are handled by other people. The company also begins adding more specialists as employees. This means that more employees are now focused on one particular aspect of the business, such as sales or technology. Gone are the days where everyone did every job in the business.

A second gauge of early growth is the development of a sales force. At this point, the business requires an ongoing marketing and sales effort if it's going to continue to grow, and most businesses create a self-sustaining sales system to address this need.

This is an exciting time for most entrepreneurs, and it certainly was for us. Our company was flourishing and growing every day, and all our employees began making real money. My own income doubled every year, from fifty thousand to one hundred thousand to well over a quarter of a million dollars a year, and the company's profits were building. In my personal life, my wife and I bought a new house in Bel Air. I felt like the future had unlimited potential, and I was living the American dream.

The company was now generating enough revenue that we could increase spending in every aspect of our business. We had grown to become a significant-sized firm in Southern California and were beginning to spread east. As we hired more people, employees began to have clearly defined roles. Slowly, our business went from a collection of generalists to a group of specialists. As we hired new employees, we looked for talented people with defined skills such as marketing or money management.

In this stage, you'll plant the seeds that determine whether your company grows or remains stagnant. Because of this, the values and culture you establish will be the cornerstone of your future. Our company hired open, can-do, results-oriented people, and they in turn hired people of similar values. Likewise, we treated people with respect and created a merit-based environment, which soon grew back upon itself and became what we stood for. Looking back, I realize that a large portion of our success was due to the decisions made at this stage. Because we developed a fantastic team of employees and salesmen who were well motivated, they loved working with us, and our company prospered and grew.

The Driving Force of a "Child," or Early Growth Business

During the early growth stage, a child's personality and traits begin to take form. The child starts to grow into who it will become as an adult. The driving force of this stage is to grow both physically and emotionally, and your business is no different. It will change and evolve, but must grow to survive.

At this point, you'll realize that a successful business requires more than just you. You'll also make some of the most important decisions regarding your company and begin to build a team of people whom you'll eventually entrust with the health of your enterprise.

Our company made some great hires, as well as some bad ones. Across the board, those that didn't work had great resumes but bad attitudes. Being part of an independent business is not for everyone, but along the way I found some common traits to look for when hiring people. I found that many of the entrepreneurs interviewed shared similar experiences. Later in the book, I'll share these hiring tactics.

As my partners and I sought employees who would thrive in our work environment, we hired people who brought passion and a strong work ethic to the business. Over time, the company was considerably transformed as each person we brought in changed the personality of our office. Everyone wanted to make an impact, so they did. At this stage we instituted "open meritocracy," which meant that we had an open-door policy: There were no secrets and those who contributed the most were rewarded the most. This created a driven, yet incredibly communicative, environment. I can't remember any employee who was a meaningful contributor to the business leaving the company at that stage. In fact, some brought their friends in to join us, and it was very exciting to put a well-oiled team together.

Why Many Independent Businesses Don't Leave This Stage

Typically a company will not evolve beyond this stage because of one of the following reasons:

- The owner does not hire well.
- The owner doesn't trust others to make decisions.

Both of these are crucial aspects of success, and will be covered at length later. I understood that our own limitations would be our biggest roadblocks to future success, and while one of my partners struggled with letting go of certain aspects of the business, over time we all found an area to focus on.

It's also crucial to understand that managing expenses at this stage can be tough. This is because hiring people is easy, but making money with them takes time. While you're waiting for additional revenue to come in, you'll have additional expenses associated with your new hires. In our case, the company's revenues grew exponentially, but so did our expenses.

We spent about four years at this stage, and our revenue increased fivefold from 1994 to 1998. It may sound impressive, but our expenses weren't too far behind. Eventually, we hit a plateau and felt for a time as if we might stay at this level. FundMinder had a great team and a wonderful working atmosphere, but our growth began to slow down. Soon we were tripping over ourselves, and the business began experiencing a significant number of client complaints for the first time.

■■■■

3. The Adolescent, or Mature Growth Stage

"I've been a client since you guys started and stuck with you through all the bad times, but this is ridiculous! I ask for a ten thousand dollar withdrawal, and you send me one thousand. I ask for a tax report, and it finally comes three weeks after the fifth time I called. Every time I try to speak to someone, they don't have time to talk."

It was 1998, and this was a recurring theme in the conversations I was having with our clients.

By now, we had become a national presence with thousands of clients across the country. We had changed our name to Centurion Capital to reflect both the broader range of investment services we offered and the larger client base we were serving. Our firm had garnered a reputation as an innovative, high-service investment company. We had glossy brochures, nice marketing campaigns, and were now being mentioned in the press. Our workforce had also grown significantly, as we were generating millions of dollars in revenues and investing most of the potential profits in order to continue the company's growth.

Yet despite our apparent success, breakdowns in quality became commonplace. Even though everyone was working hard, we weren't staying on top of day-to-day issues that popped up. We had become a service company that no longer provided reliable service. To use an analogy shared often by entrepreneurs, apples kept falling off the apple cart.

My personal experience is a classic example of what happens during the mature growth of a company, and such problems are why every business at some point must slow down and implement structure. Centurion Capital was only a few months away from a tailspin that would jeopardize the whole business. I should have picked up the warning signs, but I didn't.

■■■■

Essentially, the ability to transition from one stage of growth to the next is all about leverage. The higher the level of decisions you're involved in, the more your company will grow, but only if those decisions are made correctly. You have to delegate to qualified employees, but you must also know what is happening.

Once your business reaches the adolescent stage, it will not continue to grow unless you apply process and structure. When companies reach a certain size, they begin to get tugged in various directions, and because each part of an organization is interconnected, those parts must be coordinated in order to accomplish anything.

One aspect of this is that large businesses have accumulated a high number of clients, and each one requires care and oversight. In these situations, keeping existing clients happy can become overwhelming if you don't implement reliable procedures. Because we focused on continued growth, our clients gradually stopped receiving the reliable service to which they had become accustomed. In order to improve our business, we had to stop concentrating on growth and adjust to our new size, which meant ensuring that existing clients were satisfied with our service and reliability. It wasn't easy to resist the many opportunities that came our way during this period, but we also recognized that none of those opportunities mattered if our clients weren't happy.

At this stage, your business should build a team of managers who report on the major aspects of their departments. You should also create an executive group that helps develop a vision for the future. And because departments have to be coordinated, you need to develop procedures once you reach this stage. This is also the stage when you'll have budgets and measurement reports for each department. Such changes will undoubtedly slow things down and may drive you and your original team of employees crazy.

The Driving Force of an "Adolescent" or Mature Growth Business

As with children, your business's adolescence is a challenging time. It is when you realize that your baby, the company, is becoming an adult. This will impact you both physically and emotionally. Physically, you'll learn how to coordinate the various parts of your newly grown business, and emotionally you'll learn to become more disciplined. To put it bluntly, your company can no longer act irresponsibly. It will have to mature and begin functioning as a fully grown, adult business.

This is when your business will begin to crave structure and process, and as its entrepreneur and owner, you will have to implement that change. It will be tough, because people are resistant to change. However until your business has a way to manage decision making and growth consistently and predictably, it is not an adult business.

As Centurion Capital grew, so did our reliance on each team member. Unfortunately, some of them couldn't keep up. During this period we had several departments, each with a separate department head, and some of them always had excuses for things going wrong. Sometimes the department head was not willing to hire people more talented than they were. Other times there were bottlenecks in the workload. Also, as we started to implement budgets and measure the success of departments, some managers began pining for "the good old days." But despite these difficulties, our clients were happy with the changes and employees were appreciative of the improving structure.

Because of the difficulty of this transition, not everyone at Centurion made it through this stage. Even one of the founding partners, Werner, decided that this was no longer what he wanted. But Bob and I continued on, determined to keep the company growing to the next level.

Why Many Independent Businesses Don't Reach or Leave This Stage

During the transition to an adult company, many businesses are either sold or simply fail. Typically most businesses do not reach or surpass this stage because of one of the following reasons:

- The owner or management does not implement procedures.
- The company trips over itself and mismanages crucial issues.

For Centurion, this was our most intense period and a time of crisis. Our inferior results and lack of focus in 1998 had frustrated customers, and over a 12-month period we lost a huge number of clients. Our company was losing large streams of revenue. It was gut wrenching, particularly when we had no idea how to stop the hemorrhaging. Bob, Werner, and I weren't sure if the company would survive, and we spent countless hours discussing what we needed to do to keep the company alive.

Once things started heading south, it became obvious to everyone that something was wrong. At the time, even my best employees were worried whenever I'd ask to speak with them. The stress was affecting all of us. My hair was turning gray and falling out, while my partners were rapidly gaining weight. None of us were getting enough sleep. Work became a serious and threatening part of my home life. I can't believe my wife put up with me! After six years of good moves and good luck, it seemed quite likely that we were about to lose it all.

We knew that if we did nothing, Centurion would fail. It became easy to be creative and make some bold moves once we considered the alternative. Over the next 18 months we retooled and reinvented ourselves, coming up with innovative investment products that would be more appealing than what we'd done in the past.

Centurion was losing thousands of clients, but we believed in our solution. During those 18 months, I worked harder than I ever had in my life. I was constantly on the road telling our story while our whole team worked nonstop to turn things around. We were in a race against time, but by the end of 1999, Centurion was larger than at the end of 1998, even though it had lost a huge portion of its old clients throughout the year. We emerged from the experience a more robust company than ever before.

At this point, Werner decided to become a consultant for Centurion. He left the day-to-day operations of the business because he no longer enjoyed working with the company as much as he had. We had brought in a new partner, Jerry, to help with the operations and he brought immense operational experience and know-how to the firm.

It was humbling and gratifying to have a team of people working toward the survival of our business, and once we had successfully navigated the storm, Centurion was stronger and more mature, with happier clients and a better operating structure. We were fortunate to make it through, especially when you consider that many companies don't make it through such a challenge. But thanks to a combination of vision and belief, along with the dedication of our team and a little luck, things went our way.

If your company can survive such moments of crisis, they'll be the turning points to greater success. But I'll be the first to admit that when you're knee-deep in such trying times, it's hard to stay optimistic. When these moments occur—and from all of the interviews I conducted, they happened without exception—you must not ask yourself *if* your company will survive, but *how* it will survive.

I have never liked bureaucracy, and our team consisted mostly of people who had escaped the corporate world. Yet there we were, implementing processes and procedures like any large corporation. Mandatory weekly, monthly, and quarterly reports drove some of the folks crazy, but we knew we had no choice. We were in a highly regulated industry; it was essential that we be on top of everything. We knew Centurion could not afford one mistake. There was no other way for our business to survive, so we spent two years transitioning Centurion into a mature growth business.

■■■■

4. The "Adult" or Viable Business Stage

In early 2000, Bob and I had been working on an acquisition for several months. The particular company that we wanted to buy was a fairly large investment firm run by two well-known investment personalities. We were deciding whether or not to go ahead with the transaction.

"This is an unbelievable price. Do you have any doubts about this deal?" Bob asked me. I agreed that although we should buy the company, I was nervous about the size of the transaction, which would be over ten million dollars.

"Well, where do we get this kind of money?" we asked each other. The owners of the business we wanted to buy had not done any succession planning, which made the price quite attractive. We could make the acquisition immediately profitable and cash-flow positive. We'd made a few purchases already, but certainly nothing on this scale. To make the purchase happen, we would need to borrow a significant amount of money for the first time in the company's history. And in doing so, we were about find out whether the rest of the world thought Centurion was a solid company.

Soon, two great indicators told us that Centurion had indeed grown up. First, Union Bank gave us a line of credit for tens of millions of dollars, and second, an investment bank invested several million dollars in our firm. Both events required a high degree of due diligence and were not easy transactions to complete. However, both were successful because we operated Centurion like a much larger company than it actually was. We used lawyers and accountants who usually worked with larger companies. We also had risk-management systems that few firms our size lived with, and because of our predicament a few years earlier, we understood and had analyzed every financial aspect of the business.

With the additional capital, we were able to complete the acquisition. By the end of 2000, Centurion had over two billion dollars under management and was twice the size it had been during the crisis less than two years earlier. Our clients, employees, and managers were all happy as a result of our success. For the first time, we were able to take lengthy vacations knowing that Centurion would continue to operate well in our absence. It was the right time to sell the company.

■■■■

If your business has made it to this point, it's already grown from an idea to a small business and into a thriving enterprise. You are one of few that has navigated the turmoil and continued to compete until your business has become successful. And this is the ideal time for you to structure an exit strategy for yourself. We'll discuss this in detail later in the book, but for now, know that there is an inverse relationship between your importance to the business and the amount you will receive for it.

Simply put, this means that the more important you or any of your partners are to the day-to-day operations of your business, the less you will receive for the company when selling it. I've found this to be true both as an acquirer of businesses, and as a seller of my own. My last two years with Centurion were spent structuring the business so that it could run successfully without any of the founders being there.

Not surprisingly, this leap is one that many owners struggle with. But you'll need to eventually overcome your reluctance, because if you plan to sell, the company will be worth less if you or your partners are crucial to the business.

The Driving Force of an "Adult" or Viable Business

Just as adults need their independence, so does an adult business. At a certain point, all children leave home and continue to grow without their parents. When this happens, some parents continue to guide their children, while others allow the children to make their choices and learn their own lessons. As an entrepreneur, you'll make the same decision once you sell your business.

This doesn't mean that you can't run your business as long as you like. But regardless of how long you choose to run your business, it will not become an adult, viable enterprise until it can survive your absence. If the company would collapse without you, then it hasn't reached this stage.

During this time, my partners and I began empowering our managers and employees to take the lead on development and matters crucial to the business. Over the two-year conversion, we set up Centurion in such a way that there was no question it could survive without the founders. By the time we were done, our products and services had their own leaders, and our sales department was moving without our active involvement.

We were still involved in the strategy of the business, but whoever acquired Centurion would be in charge of that in the future. And quite frankly, they wouldn't need our assistance in creating a strategy because they would have their own vision of what the business should accomplish.

Why Many Independent Businesses Don't Reach This Stage

The key to successfully converting a business to the adult stage is typically in the hands of the owners. However, businesses that never evolve to this final stage fail to do so for one of the following reasons.

- The owner chooses not to let go of their business.
- There are not enough competent people at the top levels of the business.

Since your business must be running smoothly in order to reach the adult stage, you have the option to create a capital event for yourself once you are ready, or you can decide to keep the business indefinitely.

At Centurion, my partners and I planned to sell the business once we felt it had reached this stage. The actual process of selling the business took two years to complete.

■■■■

Throughout this book, I'll share with you the vital secrets I learned through my experience, and those that all of the entrepreneurs I interviewed found to be true. These secrets have helped many independent business owners survive the rough voyage that sinks so many businesses. Some may seem obvious to you, while others may address topics you've never thought of. But all of them will help you reach the success you deserve.

Most of all, if you are now operating, or plan to operate, your own business, remember to enjoy the ride. This is a choice that you've made. You can always go to work for a large company that will financially support you, but it will also tell you how to work and how you will be rewarded. Be aware that your company will have its own ebbs and flows, and highs and lows. Just keep moving forward, enjoy the freedom, and build something that you are proud of.

■■■■

I began this chapter with the tale of the persistent donkey. My partner and mentor, Dr. Bob, shared this tale with me when things were at their toughest, and it gave me a little extra boost. I always come back to it whenever times are challenging.

There will be moments in your own business when you'll feel like the donkey in that story, with the sand of the world constantly falling upon your head. Keep pressing and persisting, because the sunshine will feel great when you get there.

Chapter TWO

The Business Leader

What a business leader should do to create a great workplace and

maximize the potential of his company.

Vital Secret #1

Run the company like a business, not a hobby.

Vital Secret #2

Be what you want your company to become.

Vital Secret #3

Delegate, don't abdicate.

Take Your Own Direction

The Tale of the Cake-Loving Ant

It was a typically hot day in the African countryside when a nest of ants began their daily journey for food. Marching in single file, the ants headed to a nearby farmhouse, where they usually were able to find enough sugar for the whole nest.

Eventually, the train of ants arrived at the farmhouse, climbed the outside wall, crawled through a gap in the kitchen window, and continued past the sink towards the ever-present sugar bowl that lay waiting for them.

Like all ants, they had one simple rule: The ant at the front of the line led the rest of them to their meal. As such, it was up to the first ant to find enough food for everyone.

But as the troop began marching across the kitchen counter towards the sugar bowl, one of the ants in the middle of the line noticed a freshly made cake sitting on the other side of the sink. The leader, however, continued to march towards the sugar bowl.

Deciding that he'd rather have cake instead, this ant turned and headed for the prize. The other ants behind him followed, but as they crossed the sink, some began to mumble and worry about the sudden change in direction. A few even asked where they were headed as they reminded others that the sugar bowl was behind them. Ignoring the others behind him, the ant in front continued marching until they arrived at the cake.

At the end of the day, the ants returned to their nest and feasted on cake, thanks to the one ant who wanted cake instead of sugar.

The moral of the story: Only those that believe in themselves and act on their beliefs get to choose their rewards.

■■■■

The one trait shared by all successful entrepreneurs is a belief in themselves and what they want to accomplish. Although this is what sets entrepreneurs apart from average employees, confidence alone is not enough to create success.

As the owner of your company, you are its first and most important leader. You've already made the decision to believe in yourself and trust in your ability to be successful. The next step is to build upon that by setting the tone and culture that will permeate your organization as it grows. The way your business operates and works, and the qualities and values you choose to practice, will all be emulated by the people who work for you.

Good leadership comes in many forms. It is not style dependent, nor is it based on someone's personality. I have seen charismatic, personality-driven leaders succeed, and thoughtful, process-driven leaders also achieve their goals. The difference between these successful individuals and those that fail is the way they approach their businesses.

While all types of people have flourished by creating their own companies, most share common attributes in the way they guide their companies forward and the values they impart to their businesses. In this chapter, we'll learn three of the secrets essential to building a valuable business. Each one focuses on the way that you, as your company's leader, can succeed, regardless of your personality.

■■■■

Vital Secret #1

Run the enterprise like a business, not a hobby.

"But I like to design all kinds of dresses." For the past few years, Maria had been running a dress manufacturing company and had established a respectable following. In fact, a few of her dresses had even appeared on a popular TV show. The problem was that Maria's business wasn't making any money. Although her sales continued to increase, so too did the amount of money she had to spend to support her company. As the business grew, Maria had expanded to offer dozens of different variations of her popular dresses. Unsure what to do, she was meeting with a business consultant for the first time.

"Look, Maria," said the consultant, "you basically have one choice here. You can either charge more for your dresses, which would cover the increased costs, or you can have fewer designs, which would cut back some of your expenses."

"Well, I don't want to make the same few dresses over and over, and I sure can't sell my dresses for more," Maria told her. "Besides, I found some beautiful buttons that have inspired some great new designs. I think I should just wait and see what happens."

Two years later, after Maria had continued to put money into her company, she had to close shop because she was unable to make a profit. Although she felt good about what she had accomplished, she was heartbroken to let her employees go.

Maria's business failed because she treated work as a hobby and disliked the idea of running a business.

What Vital Secret #1 Should Mean to You

Although many people start companies because they have a passion for a product, an activity, or an industry, it is necessary to treat their endeavor as a business if it's going to survive. Unfortunately, many businesses fail within their first few years because the owners can't separate their personal preferences from making the best decisions for their businesses.

While it's important to enjoy what you do, remember that if your business cannot pay its bills, you will not be able to continue doing what you love. Understandably, many entrepreneurs find this balance challenging.

How to Make Vital Secret #1 Work for You

You need to do three things in order to run your company as a business and not a hobby. You must focus on learning, ask the right questions, and be "long-term" greedy rather than "short-term" greedy.

1. Focus on learning.

One of the most common traits among winning business leaders is an insatiable desire to learn. Jack Welch, the former head of General Electric, was famous for asking questions about what made each business work. It was well known among GE employees that if they sat near the CEO for a meal they would be grilled about their business, not just because he was making conversation, but also because he wanted to understand what each business was doing successfully. By doing so, he often found an operating advantage in one business that could be applied to other divisions of GE.

Smart entrepreneurs keep learning. Meet with people who have their own companies. Join associations and attend forums to learn from your peers. Find out what has worked for them and what hasn't. Learn the realities of your particular industry and pick the minds of those who are successful. Speak to people who work with your competitors or potential competitors, especially those whose companies are bigger than yours. Think of this activity as receiving a free education from those who are more knowledgeable and more experienced.

2. Ask the right questions.

Today, Socrates is considered one of the wisest philosophers in the history of humankind, yet his knowledge came from asking the right questions in order to get the best answers.

Whenever an important decision must be made, it is essential to ask the right questions. A key part of this means asking questions in the right way. You'll never get the right answer if you don't frame your question accurately. Global questions get far less accurate responses than specific questions.

For example, if you owned several retail stores and called each manager to ask how business was going, the answer would probably be something vague, such as "Okay," "So-so" or "Pretty good." This type of response is not very valuable, since it doesn't tell you anything specific. Instead, if you asked those same managers how many sales have occurred so far this month and what they anticipate for the remainder of the month, you'd get specific answers that you could act on.

If you ask these kinds of targeted questions often enough, your employees will begin thinking about the business the same way you do. This will help them to focus on the issues that matter to you. What you must do is learn what is important for your company so that you know what questions to ask.

Also, try to view your business as its own entity and make decisions based on what is best for the business rather than what is best for you. One of the most common underlying questions you should ask yourself is "What is best for the business?" You would be surprised how seldom that question is asked in a typical independent company.

3. **Focus on being long-term greedy, not short-term greedy.** Unlike a large public corporation, whose constant focus is on quarterly results, you have the significant advantage of being able to think long-term. Because of this, you can make shifts that might negatively impact profits in the short-term, but have a hugely beneficial impact on the long-term prospects and growth of your company.

For example, you might decide to introduce a new product or enter into a new market, and spend significant profits in your endeavor to grow and be more successful over time. Owning a privately held company is similar to owning real estate in that neither gets valued every day. This allows you to make improvements for the long-term without worrying about the daily fluctuations of your company's value—something that is a constant concern for corporations.

In short, making decisions based on what is right for the health of the company is crucial to the vitality of your organization. Since the business leader sets the tone for the rest of the employees, you are responsible for creating a healthy culture within your business.

■■■■

Vital Secret #2

Be what you want your company to become.

Suzie met Mike thirty years ago. At the time, he ran a software company with hundreds of employees. She was interviewing with Mike for a position at the company, and had been warned that he could be a tough fellow. After an exciting and challenging interview, she was hired. Suzie was soon given a big design project to lead, and over time she and Mike fell in love and got married. Together, they built the company up to 1,400 employees and created a great workplace. Throughout it all, Mike was the undisputed leader of the company. He set the vision, led the team, and was almost like an evangelist in his belief in the company and what it was doing. He was confident, honest, hard working, and incredibly vibrant. Because employees loved him and emulated his example, the company flourished. Suzie, meanwhile, worked behind the scenes as his anchor and sounding board.

Unfortunately, Mike passed away suddenly in his mid-forties. Suzie was heartbroken. . The employees wanted her to run the company, but she didn't want to be in charge by herself. She knew that the company was a reflection of Mike and that she could not be like him. The people who ran the company wanted to maintain the same relationship they'd had with Mike. Suzie realized that although Mike had enjoyed running the business, she did not. She knew that this would be reflected in the company and that over time it was not what was best.

After much consideration, Suzie decided to sell the company. She did extremely well financially in the process, and many of her employees became millionaires over time After five years of relaxation, she began a new business of her own.

■■■■

What Vital Secret #2 Should Mean to You

To see this rule in action, you need look no further than some of the largest and best-known companies in the world. Whether it's the success of Warren Buffett's Berkshire Hathaway or the failure of Ken Lay's Enron, the culture of a business reflects its executives. This is intensified in small businesses, which makes this rule doubly true for you. Simply put, your business is like a mirror that will reflect your actions and values, whether good or bad. The people you hire, the way they work, and the values the company practices are all set by you, the owner. All of your confidence and insecurities will be reflected in the way the company works.

Business leaders who set a positive example for their company exhibit five traits. This is not meant to be an exhaustive list—every entrepreneur adds their own ideas and values—but these five were the most commonly cited among all the entrepreneurs I interviewed. They are ranked in order.

1. Integrity

Integrity means doing what you say you will do, and, if in doubt, always doing the right thing. Colin Powell is a great example of a man who embodies integrity. He says what he intends to do and then does it. His actions have demonstrated a willingness to do the right thing no matter what. When he disagrees with the administration he serves, he says so. Powell has served under both Democratic and Republican presidents, and even in times of scandal or upheaval, he has been consistently viewed as a pillar of integrity.

Poor integrity is a quick way to destroy any business, but for small businesses, this is even more so. If your employees see you as fickle and question your ethics, they either will not work with you for long or they will follow your lead and behave dishonestly. However, if they see that you consistently set an honest and trustworthy example, they will realize that anything less is not tolerated.

2. Persistence

Persistence is the cornerstone of every successful leader. Consider Sir Winston Churchill, Great Britain's Prime Minister during World War II. His country was being besieged by the Nazis, and there was almost no way the English could win. Yet he persevered, pushing the people of Britain to great levels. He would not give up under any condition, and when he gave his famous "we will never surrender" speech, everyone knew he meant it. Great Britain supported him because they knew that he would never give up.

As an entrepreneur, you'll have to overcome all kinds of obstacles, but through them all, you must find a way to keep going. No one has the incentive to keep your business moving forward that you do. A culture of persistence and determination is essential for a small business to succeed.

3. Optimism

Optimism means always believing that there is a solution to whatever challenge is in front of you. President Franklin D. Roosevelt was just such a person. He made the United States feel that every problem had a solution, and that he could rise to any challenge. Roosevelt took over the White House in the midst of the worst depression in the country's history, yet he restored American pride, confidence, and most importantly, hope. His immortal speech, stating, "We have nothing to fear but fear itself," epitomized his belief in the great opportunities ahead for the country.

The key to optimism is always asking "How?" rather than "Why?": "How do we fix this?" "How do we avoid this issue in the future?" "How do I turn this into a positive?" There will be many instances when you will be presented with problems. How you deal with them will be evaluated and copied, so remain optimistic. The key to an optimistic business mind is to view every problem as an opportunity to grow and learn.

4. Adaptability

Adaptability means accepting change and adjusting to it. A great example of this can be seen in Ted Williams, the last major league baseball player to bat over .400. Williams was the most consistent hitter in baseball history, and the key to his success is linked to his adaptability. A game in which Williams's Boston Red Sox were matched against the Cleveland Indians highlights this perfectly. Williams was known as a right-field hitter, so Lou Boudreau, the Indians' shortstop, told his team to cheat right (which in baseball terms, means shift to the right). Williams watched the team shift, then belted the ball solidly to left field. He had worked on adjusting his hitting to ensure that he didn't become predictable, and it paid off. Without the ability to adapt to each challenge, no player could bat with the consistency Williams did.

The same is true for business owners. In a small business, things change often, and you must be able to accept change as a part of life. Your company should be able to make changes quickly. This is a major advantage you have over large corporations—make the most of it.

5. Humility

Humility means keeping grounded. Warren Buffett, one of the world's wealthiest men and most respected financial minds, is a great example of humility. Despite his wealth, power, and influence, you'd be hard pressed to find a trace of arrogance in him. As any interview with Buffett demonstrates, he gives credit to those around him and never assumes that he is always right.

Likewise, you should strive to be confident, but not arrogant. The moment you think you know all there is to know, the business world will undoubtedly bring you back to earth. I've seen numerous examples of entrepreneurs who thought their companies were bullet proof, only to find out that they were not. Being humble keeps you always striving to improve, and aware of competition. After all, the business race is a marathon—running the first ten miles well doesn't mean you've won.

■■■■

How to Make Vital Secret #2 Work for You

There are three ways to be what you want your company to become. You need to imitate the best, make a list and evaluate yourself, and maintain a sense of humor.

1. Imitate the best.

Simply put, find someone you respect and imitate him. This has worked for many business owners on two separate levels. On a personal level, act the way you think someone you respect would act. Some people imitate their grandfather, others a business icon. For example, Gary, the owner of a successful trucking company, was understandably nervous about taking over the business from his father. Even though he'd been involved with trucking for several years, he still felt a little apprehensive. Gary went in that first day thinking that he would emulate some of the traits of his father, a man he always respected and to whom he felt kinship. When faced with tough issues he would ask himself, "What would he do?" The answers came easily. This gave him guidance and strength and helped him to continue the prosperity of his father's trucking business.

Second, with respect to your business, it should function the way a company you respect would. For this, it's important to emulate a business that is bigger than yours. In the course of my company's history, we consistently shifted our benchmark and copied bigger companies as we grew. This process is called modeling and is valuable to your company's growth.

2. Make a list and evaluate yourself.

Draw up a list of the five virtues listed previously and add others that are important to you. Keep the list handy and set aside a regular time to review the list and consider how you're doing. Also, use this time to find out how the company is doing. A good way to do this is to ask some of your employees how the company rate on these issues.

3. Maintain a sense of humor.

Many business leaders have the ability to defuse the tensest situations with a sense of humor. The ability to "lighten up" an intense situation is crucial. This is true whether it's a negotiation that is particularly challenging, or a delicate and serious situation.

The ability to maintain an appropriate sense of humor without trivializing important situations has proven to be a lifesaver for many business leaders. It always surprises me how many successful entrepreneurs have a great ability to laugh. Throughout my career, I have seldom seen a successful businessperson who takes themselves too seriously.

A nice example of this came from the owner of an investment company whose business we were buying. We'd been negotiating for some time and the last topic we had to resolve was his ongoing income stream. "Well," I said, "after the price we've agreed to, it's almost impossible for us to work in an ongoing consulting salary of the size you're talking." The moment was tense, since we were at the tipping point, that moment when a deal goes one way or another. The owner looked at us and in a deadpan voice said, "Well, guys, either I give you the keys to the shop and a list of the local restaurants, or I show you where you should order from. You decide." We all laughed and eventually came to an agreement that worked for all of us.

Vital Secret #3

Delegate, don't abdicate.

"One thousand nine hundred and twenty. Do you know what that is?" Doug asked me. "It's the number of hours you work in one year. If you work a forty-hour week for forty-eight weeks, it's all the time you have in a year to make money. If you want to make a million dollars a year, you have to earn five hundred and ten dollars per hour, every hour, and that ain't easy."

Doug is a very successful financial planner. Starting with nothing, he built his own company over several years. As Doug explains it, he started with a few thousand dollars and not a single client. But in ten years he *built a firm with over $100 million under management. He is one of the best advisors I've ever met, and his employees love working with him. He explained to me the key to his success.*

"I never forget what my time is worth," he told me. "I always want to work less, and I want to do what I love to do. I love to meet with my clients, I love to ski, and I love going to my cabin with my wife. Every year I work less, but every year I earn more, and there is only one way I could do that. You have to work with people who are very talented, and they have to consistently pick up your work and do it as well as you do, if not better. If I didn't have a great team that I can trust, it simply couldn't happen. Of course, I always speak to my clients, and they always let me know if something's not working right."

What Vital Secret #3 Should Mean to You

This secret boils down to something we all know is true: Time is your most valuable commodity. If you spend your days doing $5.00-an-hour work, it's going to be almost impossible for your business to grow. As your company expands, so should the value of the work you are involved in. And the only way to increase the value of the work you do is by hiring talented people to whom you can delegate. Conversely the lower the level of work you do, the less your company will grow.

The people you hire and entrust to pick up some of the responsibilities should be good at what they do. Ideally they should be even better at it than you are, but it's not essential. This is a tough dilemma for many entrepreneurs because they often worry that employees can't do the job as well as they can. Usually, these business owners don't delegate, or if they do, they might micromanage everything and lose all of the leverage they should be getting from their employees.

To show why it's okay if your employees don't do things quite as well as you, consider this example.

Imagine that Steve, a business owner, is considering hiring a sales force. He's worried that no one can sell his products as well as he can, and assumes that anyone he hires will be only half as good at selling the products. If Steve spends half his working time selling his products, should he hire a dedicated full-time salesperson?

Yes, because even if the person is only half as good as Steve, this employee will make the same amount of sales as Steve would have.

Think about it. If Steve hires a new salesperson, that individual will be spending the entire workday selling, twice as much time as Steve is currently spending. So the net effect is that sales will remain the same even if the new hire is only half as good as Steve. Now, this also means that five people only half as good as Steve could do five times the amount of sales that Steve does by himself. This is assuming the new hires are only half as good as he is! There's another major benefit to hiring a sales force. By doing so, Steve now has more time to work on other things because he has freed up half of his workday.

Of course, this simple example doesn't consider the costs associated with an employee. However, it does illustrate the point that since you are performing many functions, people with less skill can still make meaningful contributions to your company because they are spending more time than you in their area of focus.

Whether it's sales or any other aspect of the business, this little example can be a reminder of the importance of leverage, as well as of delegating responsibilities. So put your time to its optimum use and remember its value.

I should point out, however, that there is an important second part to this vital secret. Delegating and abdicating are different. Abdicating is handing off without supervision, and you cannot afford to do this. Anyone you hand off work to is not going to have as much at stake as you do, so always stay aware of what the different components of your business are doing.

Basically, there are two ways to do this. First, you can require an ongoing report from the person you've delegated work to, or you can choose to have an ongoing dialogue with your clients. Client feedback, from both those who buy your good or services, and those who have stopped buying from you, can be a magnificent way to hear how things are going.

How to Make Vital Secret #3 Work for You

In order to delegate without abdicating, you need to do four things: Analyze what your time is worth, analyze how you spend your time, prioritize your work list, and meet with your clients.

1. **Analyze what your time is worth.**

   Divide the income you'd like to make a year by 1,920 and you'll get an idea of the average value that your work hour should be worth. For example, if you'd like to make $500,000 per year, your time must be worth $260 per hour ($500,000 ÷ 1920 = $260). This is important because it will help you assess what kind of work you should be doing. Clearly time spent making photo copies or fixing phone lines is not worth $260 an hour. If you keep the dollar amount in your mind you will go through your day noticing the work you do that lowers your income and productivity.

2. **Analyze how you spend your time.**

   Create a list of how you spend your time during the working day, and track yourself for a week. The best way to do this is to keep a journal and write down what you do throughout each day. There's no need to be scientific; simply put your activities into general categories such as accounting, administration, and so on. Once the week is over, analyze the results. You'll probably be surprised by what you find. In fact, don't be shocked if more than half your time is spent on trivial work. Many people who have gone through this exercise find that no less than 60 percent of their time is spent in trivial or unproductive work or lengthy distractions. Now that you know what you're doing with your day, you can set about improving your time management.

3. **Prioritize your list.**

   Using the journal, prioritize your daily activities by their importance to your business. As you do this, ask yourself what you'd pay someone else, per hour, to do that same task. Once you've prioritized everything you do, begin looking at the items with the lowest priorities. Which of these jobs could be done by someone else? Think about delegating those tasks that are the cheapest to do and can be easily delegated. If you decided that you could find someone else to do administrative work (typing letters, making copies and scheduling meetings), imagine what you could do with your free time. If you freed up 10 hours a week, how many sales could you make that would never have occurred? Typically if you can redirect that time to something more valuable to the business, you will pay for the additional expense of a new employee very quickly. Sometimes hiring is not even necessary. One entrepreneur who went through this exercise simply farmed out several of his responsibilities to his five employees. He found that they appreciated the trust and that he could get a lot more done.

4. Meet with your clients.

When Lou Gerstner took over IBM, it was a struggling computer company. Instead of looking for innovative products and the "next big thing," he spent his first six months on the job meeting clients outside the office. Throughout his career as CEO, Gerstner continued leaving the office to see clients every quarter, and as a result, IBM flourished under his direction.

There should never be a protracted period of time during which you don't speak to your clients, and the bigger your company is, the more you should listen. Many of your clients will have concerns, so ask them what two things they would do to improve your company and listen objectively. Write all of their suggestions down. Next, ask them for their two favorite things about working with your company, and write those down. As you begin to compile a list, you'll probably be surprised at the vastly different perceptions your clients have about your company. But as you talk to them, you should start to learn what is working at your business and what is not. Eventually, your list will tell you what you should be spending your time to improve or change.

At the end of the day, leading your own business means always leveraging yourself and your staff, making sure the business keeps reaching its targets.

We began this chapter with the tale of the cake-loving ant who had the courage to risk failure in order to reach his own treasure. As an entrepreneur, you've already made a move that few are ever willing to make—you decided to take care of yourself. No one working for you has taken that risk so do not expect them to understand some of the issues that you'll go through. It is essential, however, that everyone at your company believe in your ability as a leader, or it will be nearly impossible to keep your team on track and productive. Keep your eyes on the cake, and keep marching!

Chapter THREE

The Culture

Setting a winning mindset, and creating a productive,

enjoyable, and loyal work environment.

Vital Secret #4

Put people first, make them feel special.

Vital Secret #5

Run your company as an open meritocracy.

Work Together

The Fight Between the Lion and the Tribe

Deep in the jungle of Africa lived a peaceful tribe. Its people were happy, for they ate well, danced often, and lived in harmony with nature. They grew their own vegetables and kept goats and cattle for milk, meat, and hide. Their lives were tranquil and peaceful.

One day one of the tribe's young men was tending the goats, when he noticed one was missing. He ran back to the elders and told them about the missing beast. Upon hearing this news, the elders agreed that the goat had escaped by jumping over a rickety wood fence the tribe had built.

The next day, one of the tribe's young men noticed that a cow was missing, but that one of its legs had been left behind. This time, the elders concluded that a lion must be the cause of these problems. The tribe had seen this occur once before, many years ago before they built the fence.

That night, the tribe's best fighter lay in wait for the lion, holding his best spear in hand. Soon he watched the lion pounce into the corral and begin chasing after the tribe's animals. As soon as the tribesman jumped out to surprise the lion, it ran toward the village. The warrior chased the lion, screaming to alert his tribe to the charging beast. The other men of the tribe grabbed their spears and soon chased the lion out of the village and up the hill. Once the animal was far gone, the elders declared victory and the tribe sang and danced on their long walk back.

Yet when the tribe returned home, all their cattle and goats were gone. While they were chasing the lion, the rest of the pride had come in and taken their animals.

The moral of the tale: The group with the most focus gets the treasures.

■■■■

All companies have a business culture, and they typically reflect the collection of people that are assembled together. In many independent businesses, the culture just happens and is not purposefully developed. As we mentioned in the previous chapter, it always mirrors the business owner's own values, since they hire employees with similar personalities and create a mindset they are comfortable with. However, some entrepreneurs deliberately commit their team to certain standards and codes of conduct.

This means that the way many successful companies act and behave is thought out, planned, and developed. The best way to illustrate the importance of culture is to ask yourself what your feelings are about the way your company is and what it stands for.

To better explain, let's consider a few examples. What do you feel when you think of IBM? The Ritz Carlton? Nordstrom's? Now try the same thing, but consider companies within the same industry. How are Southwest Airlines and United Airlines different? Now take this idea one step further and attempt to describe the culture of a local business, such as your deli, dry cleaner, or hairdresser. Every company leaves an impression on its customers. All companies inherently have a culture, but those that focus on theirs have a huge advantage over competitors.

To begin, it's necessary to first understand how your business is viewed. Ask yourself, "What do my clients think and feel about our company? What do they see as our way of doing business?" Regardless of whether or not you think you have a culture, you already do. The real question is, how would you like to be perceived?

There are as many cultures as there are companies. However, the secrets in this chapter focus on those crucial things that an independent business needs to do to thrive in a competitive landscape. After all, you're competing with huge conglomerates as well as other smaller entrepreneurs.

As you work to develop and strengthen your culture, it might also help to ask yourself, "What would make my clients want to work with us more than with my major competitors?"

Vital Secret #4

Put people first, make them feel special.

Matt became CEO of the family business at 28 years old. His grandfather had started a bakery in 1928, and it had become one of the largest independent bakeries in the country. "I'd gone to law school and gotten my MBA," explained Matt, "and had come back to work when my father stepped down. Even though I hadn't been working there in a while, I had helped out in the past by fixing problems and gaining business experience."

"My father," he explained, "was an expert at planting a seed in a person and watching it grow. He would instill abilities and confidence in people, and then watch as they improved themselves, and the business in the process."

"Over twenty-five percent of our employees have worked for us over twenty years, and we promote from within. So really, the business is like a family. But a specific example of this growth is when one of our best bakers wanted to go into sales. He was looking to advance his career, but we didn't want to lose him as a great baker and producer. So my partner at the time jokingly told him that if he learned to speak Greek, he could have the job."

"Three months later, the baker came into our offices and began speaking Greek," laughed Matt. "He'd asked one of our customers to teach him, and he'd learned the language in three months. The best part is that once we gave him the job in sales, he went on to become a supervisor and continued his learning. As you can imagine he's a very happy employee. Today he speaks five languages."

■■■■

What Vital Secret #4 Should Mean to You

Of all the advantages you have against larger companies, your best asset is your business's ability to treat people uniquely. By their very nature, large enterprises need to create mass solutions and boilerplate answers to problems because of their size and scale. Since they are working with so many clients, large corporations cannot afford to spend time customizing solutions for each individual. The economics of their business dictate that they spend time and energy on the "sweet-spots" of their business. In other words, these businesses concentrate on improving their services for their ideal customer and target market. You, on the other hand, can create a people-centric company that focuses on people as individuals, not as another number to make money on. This is one of the major reasons that people would rather work with a smaller company. They think they will be more important to a smaller company than they might be to a bigger one, and so they will be looked after better.

Every company must deal with three key constituents: customers, suppliers and employees. To better understand them, let's compare how large corporations typically deal with each constituent to how smaller companies address them, and determine where the advantages lie.

The Customer

The Large Corporation

What works: Large companies typically focus on providing consistent products and services for a middle-of-the-road, or average, client. They also want to provide quick solutions as cheaply as possible to anyone who has a standard need.

What doesn't: Corporations are not very good at dealing with variations of customers. Any difficulty or troubleshooting that doesn't fall into an average or "normal" range also creates problems for the company and client.

The Independent Company

What works: Independent businesses can offer customized solutions and service to their clients. They can have a much higher level of personal touch, and since there are fewer employees, it's usually easier for a customer to reach a knowledgeable person when problems arise.

What doesn't: Yet small business sometimes provide inconsistent solutions and unreliable service. Often, more time is needed to solve basic problems, which can be costly for the company and for the client.

At some point, we've all experienced the frustration of calling a big company about a problem, only to be read a script, then be endlessly transferred from person to person. Remember the last time you tried calling your phone company or car leasing firm with a complex question? Usually, scripts are used in these situations because the person answering your questions doesn't know how to fix your problem. As customers, we often pick up on this, and even though you'll eventually speak to someone who can help you, getting to that specialist takes a very long time.

This happens because the majority of problems the company addresses are similar in nature, so the business develops a "canned" solution and is able to provide the answer in a cheap manner by having someone read you the solution. This process is called "mass customization," and it's a way to provide what appear to be custom solutions that are in fact mass-produced.

What we all enjoy about this, even though we might not appreciate it at the time, is that for every frustrating call, there are many that go smoothly and far quicker than they might otherwise.

As an entrepreneur, your challenge is to provide quick, consistent solutions to the most frequent concerns that your customers have. But since you also have the advantage of being able to provide a customized solution, you should be able to do that as well. Whatever your business, having the ability to treat your customer as a person instead of a number is a huge advantage that large companies can seldom match. As your business grows, this balance will become much more difficult to manage. But regardless, you should strive to remain focused on this, because this is a key reason many potential clients would rather work with a smaller company.

The Supplier

The Large Corporation

What works: Larger companies have an advantage when it comes to suppliers because they have the ability to negotiate prices, terms and conditions. They can squeeze suppliers in many ways, but they typically get what they want when they want it.

What doesn't: Because of this, some suppliers to large corporations get frustrated with the way they are treated. They have to constantly lower their prices and offer conditions such as free delivery in order to keep the account.

The Independent Company

What works: Independent companies often have a friendly relationship with suppliers.

What doesn't: Unfortunately, independent companies are often treated as second-class citizens. The smaller you are, the worse you'll typically fare with a supplier. Higher prices and less reliable service are common among suppliers to small businesses.

This is one area of business where bigger is better. Large corporations can negotiate prices that most independent businesses cannot, as well as negotiate terms and conditions in contracts. Therefore, they have the ability to get products and services at a fraction of your cost and receive them in a more predictable manner than you would. Although suppliers might prefer working with you because you aren't as demanding as a corporation, being small seldom helps when problems arise. As your business grows, you can and should increasingly demand more of your suppliers.

Employees

The Large Corporation

What works: Large corporations typically provide their employees with excellent benefits and have well-defined and established policies for almost every issue. They also offer predictable career paths for all employees, and working with a known brand can be very appealing to some workers.

What doesn't: There is little true job security in a large company, there are limited open-ended wealth-making opportunities, and some employees dislike having predictable career paths.

The Independent Company

What works: Employees at an independent company are often able to make an impact. They typically have open-ended career opportunities, and often the potential for growing wealth-making opportunities. Flexibility on work policies and procedures is also a big plus.

What doesn't: Working for an unknown company and brand can be challenging for some employees, and smaller companies often have lesser benefits than larger businesses. There is also a common perception that jobs with small businesses are "riskier" than at large companies.

At the higher levels of management, there is typically a significant difference between the large company employee and the independent company employee. However, at the staff level, employees are often similar. After all, a receptionist at a small doctor's office is doing a similar job to the receptionist at a large practice with twenty doctors.

People are usually attracted to smaller companies because of their flexible environment. For example, most small businesses let employees dress less conservatively than large corporations, keep different hours, and take personal time when necessary. An employee also has greater potential to further his or her career and income more quickly in a smaller company. There is a perception that employees at a small company have a better balance of work and life than their counterparts at large businesses, and I've noticed this to be true, even as a company grows. All of the business owners I interviewed said they wanted to make working at their company a unique experience.

However, an independent business has one huge advantage, and it is that the most talented employees want to make a difference in a business. Unlike employees at corporations who accept their role within the company, your best potential employees want to be part of something meaningful. Just as a large company has a significant advantage when dealing with suppliers, you have the advantage when it comes to hiring talented people once it is evident your company will survive.

As I spoke with entrepreneurs for this book, I learned that they were almost always able to hire whomever they wanted. This occurred for two reasons. First, entrepreneurs can be creative in offering terms to potential employees, and second, new employees realized that they would have the ability and latitude to make a difference in the business. Entrepreneurs are also able to offer talented potential employees ownership interest that could potentially make them wealthy over time.

So when compared to a large corporation, your business has an advantage with employees, and can have a significant advantage with clients. Always remember that you can do what a large company cannot, which is to treat people as individuals. Embedding this into your culture will create an important difference between your company and competitors.

■■■■

How to Make Vital Secret #4 Work for You

You must do four things to put people first and make them feel special. You need to find out what your company culture, set the example, create a mission statement, and give positive reinforcement.

1. Identify your current company culture.

The best way to do this is to ask your employees and customers to give you no more than five words that describe your company. For clients, present this as a contest, and have a raffle drawing to give prizes to randomly selected contributors. Follow the same exercise for your employees, asking them to describe what it's like to work at your company.

Once you collect this information from employees and customers, write down the most commonly used descriptions. The answers you get from customers will tell you how your company is perceived, while employee responses will give you insight into your workplace.

If this perception is different than you believe to be true, it will still take a lot of time and determination to change it. This idea was shared with me several years ago, and after the first time our company conducted such a survey, we made sporadic spot checks to see if perceptions of our business had changed over time. Although some people's opinions definitely changed over the years, many stayed the same.

2. Set the example.

Nothing will do more to create an environment that puts people first than a leader who lives and breathes those ideals. It takes only a few instances when you take extra care of a customer or an employee to set the tone for your business. Whether it's calling someone personally when your company makes a mistake, or visiting employees at a hospital if they get sick, changing perceptions can happen relatively quickly if you stick to it. Maintain that behavior consistently and over time, and you'll be recognized as a people-centered company. Once employees and clients tell others that your business "really cares about me," you'll have come a long way to getting there.

3. Create the right kind of mission statement.

Many businesses develop a mission statement. But remember a mission statement is most important in telling your employees what you stand for. After all if you do what you say you'll do, your clients will know what you stand for by your actions. To start, write down what your business will do for customers in a simple paragraph of 35 words or less. Include the basics, such as what the company actually does and how you will do it. Try to keep the language simple and accessible. If you find that you're coming up with longer mission statements, determine the core of what you want to accomplish and how you'd like to do it.

For example, if you were writing a mission statement for a dry-cleaner, you might say you want to be courteous, respectful, and responsive, and put the customer first. However, if you asked yourself why you want to do these things, you would come up with something that is more appealing to the client. In this case, the dry cleaning company strives to be all those things because they want customers to have a good experience. Therefore, you would probably end up with something like, "We will take care of our customer's clothes as if they were our own, and will strive to ensure that every client has a positive experience with us."

That might be a lofty mission statement for a dry-cleaner, but it would certainly shape the culture of that business. The statement would give the business a benchmark by which to measure its success, as well as the achievements of its employees over time.

4. Give positive reinforcement.

Every quarter, recognize an employee for an action that exemplifies the values you want to endorse and support in your business. This should be done with fanfare and pride, and you should give a meaningful reward to that employee.

At our company, my partners and I would recognize the employee of the quarter in front of his or her peers and explain that we appreciated what they had done. Afterwards, the employee got to choose from a few prizes. If the employee was a Los Angeles Lakers fan, we might include Lakers tickets alongside other things we knew that person liked. It became something we all looked forward to, because everyone enjoyed watching the star employee agonize over the selection. Most of the business owners we spoke to had similar programs to recognize positive actions by employees. One company had a program for recognizing something that had happened over the past month that best reflected the company's values. All involved were rewarded in public. That's a great way to show all of your employees the way you want them to act.

Creating a culture centered around people is crucial to your ability to stand out as an independent business. Your culture will serve as one of your biggest attractors when competing with others, but only if you practice what you preach.

The biggest benefit to this secret is that as your company gains a reputation for care and concern, so too will its ability to keep loyal clients and employees.

■■■■

Vital Secret #5

Run your company as an open meritocracy.

A good example of an open meritocracy came from Ron, a born and bred entrepreneur. Before he was old enough to drive, Ron had already created two businesses, selling gumballs through antique refurbished gumball machines and washing windows for businesses and homes in his town. But after completing law school, Ron continued following his entrepreneurial heart. He created a law practice that became one of the nation's largest criminal defense law firms with over 300 attorneys, before he sold it in 2003.

"We have a call center that handles incoming calls from potential clients who need representation. Our management ranks the call center team each month, and groups each employee into a top third, a middle third, and a bottom third. When we interview people for our call center, we ask them if they think they will fall into the top third of producers. Of course, most insist they will, to which we say, 'Good, we've got a common understanding, then.' We also make it clear that if an employee falls in that bottom third three months in a row, they're likely to be let go."

Ron also cites public display of these lists as essential to treating everyone on an equal footing. "We hang the list on the wall where everyone can see it," he explained. "We also hang up our sales goals, as well as where we are in terms of a monthly goal, and make notes of employees who are doing exceptionally well. We celebrate success and acknowledge failure."

"Everything is out in the open," he explained. "Not everyone likes this, but it's mostly the lesser achievers that dislike it. Those employees that are actually doing well love it."

■■■■

What Vital Secret #5 Should Mean to You

Imagine working at a company where your opinions were heard, where you understood how your work contributed to the success of the company, and where your efforts were rewarded and recognized. Providing those things to your employees is what open meritocracy is about.

Running an open meritocracy is crucial to a small, independent business for two reasons. First, there's the benefit of teamwork. Creating a work environment where everyone is trying to accomplish the same thing with passion and conviction can help to make the voyage much more rewarding and immensely more pleasurable.

Second, there's the benefit of accelerated problem recognition and correction. Since you don't have the size and scale of a large corporation, your business can't afford any surprises. Having an open meritocracy can help you identify challenges to your business early on and will ensure that problems will be addressed quickly and effectively.

To better understand this concept, let's look at each of the words "open" and "meritocracy" in detail, and consider what they mean to you as the owner of a business.

Open

In this concept, the use of one word is a shortening of the term "open management." Open management is the process of creating a sharing and communicative environment within your company, and there are three parts to having an "open management" structure:

1. **Open reporting.** This means management openly discusses with their staff such business issues as financials, strategic plans, goals and targets, and company challenges. This also means having ongoing updates when the whole team can evaluate how the company is doing.

2. **Open communications.** Openness also means that everyone practices an open-door policy, especially the CEO. The goal is to create a spirit of approachability and sharing.

3. Open evaluations. This should also mean that everyone knows where they stand and which departments are making commitments or missing them.

Once everyone is comfortable with an "open management" structure, communication typically flows more easily. Employees know that they can approach anyone with concerns and questions, and that they are a part of something where everyone knows what is happening.

Implementing an environment of open management can also help reduce stress and expenses. For example, a mail clerk who regularly sent packages via Fed-Ex noticed the financial impact this was having on company costs, so he checked to see if some items could be sent via regular mail. Because everyone was aware of what his division spent on mail, he saved the company significantly on mail costs.

Sharing all information creates real changes to a management team. Their increasing knowledge and understanding of financials come with huge benefits to the company, and since they actually help allocate the annual budget, it becomes easier for every department to stick to their forecast.

For example, at Centurion Capital we added a professional sales manager. Tom was a far better salesman than I'd ever been, and he knew how to motivate and create actions much more effectively than I did. He set sales targets and knew how to reach them, but he needed improvements in the company to hit those goals. It was necessary for us to be open to changes managers suggested along the way we had to try doing things differently from how we'd always conducted business in the past.

Meritocracy

Simply put, meritocracy is a meritbased culture. It's the opposite of a government where seniority ranks, and in a meritocracy, ability and execution are how people climb the business ladder.

For example, think of a professional sports team. Regardless of the team or sport, it's accepted that some players are more talented than others, and that everyone plays a different position and is crucial to the team's success. The more talent and ability a player brings to the team, the greater responsibility and rewards he or she receives.

This doesn't mean that you can't have happy employees at every level of your business, but your high achievers will have the potential to work their way up. This is essential because nothing attracts talented people more than giving them the potential to flourish and grow. It's also appealing to ambitious employees because they will be able to improve both their incomes and resumes over time.

In short, practicing open meritocracy means you need to be comfortable with having your employees know a great deal about your business. You'll also need to create an environment where people earn success rather than expect it because of their history.

How to Make Vital Secret #5 Work for You

You must do five things to create an open meritocracy. You need to open your door, share the details, accept mistakes, reward superior talent, and have fun.

1. Open your door.

Begin by letting your employees know that your door is always open to them. Have them come in occasionally, so they'll feel comfortable meeting with you in your office. Tell your employees that closed doors are for truly confidential situations. Ensure that those working with you also have an open door and an approachable mindset.

2. Share the details.

You should also start setting quarterly targets that everyone can strive to reach. Create a bonus based upon reaching those targets, regardless of whether they are sales-based, profits-based or expenses-based. Track everyone's progress throughout the quarter.

At many companies, the partners keep track of quarterly goals and update them weekly in a public area like a lunchroom. If they hit their targets or exceed them, everyone wins. In the process, employees become more conscious about the details of the business.

3. Accept mistakes.

Let employees know that challenges and mistakes are a part of business, and that it's impossible for everything to be perfect. Tell your staff that if they are concerned about something, they should mention it immediately, rather than wait. This mindset helps many companies immensely, because service and sales staff become comfortable letting management know when there are real issues that need to be addressed.

4. Recognize and reward superior talent.

Not everyone is the same, and not every employee's contributions are equal. Just as nothing demoralizes an individual more than comparing them to others, nothing will lift them more than recognizing and rewarding their unique talents. However, you should create an environment where results and contributions to the company are what get employees ahead.

Your most capable employees should be given more to do, but you'll also need to make certain they do not misuse their increased responsibilities. Building a reputation as a company that rewards talent will bring you more talent, and having everyone review the numbers in an open fashion will provide proof of why certain people are getting promotions or raises. It helps to insulate the company from accusations of favoritism.

5. Have fun.

It's important to create a fun environment because it will have a positive impact on both your employees and customers. At ABC auctions, a huge and thriving auctioneering firm, the owner created a booster club to devise ways to spend the $300 each month to boost morale. It was the club's job to create and carry out enjoyable events every few weeks. Among the activities planned for the business were pizza parties, go-cart races, "King for a Day" themes, and other contests. These events made employees feel appreciated and had a great impact with minimal expense.

Turning your company into an open meritocracy is an ongoing challenge that will make a huge contribution to your business. It will create a strong team where your less capable employees will likely feel quite uncomfortable, but everyone will feel challenged and fairly rewarded. I can think of no secret that had a bigger impact on the quality of our team and culture over the years.

The fight between the lion and the tribe illustrates how the lions' singular focus of capturing the livestock overwhelmed the more ambivalent tribe.

The Group with the higher focus gets the treasures.

Your business can either be the lion, or the tribe. You have the choice of shaping your culture, or letting it evolve by itself. Unfortunately, if you choose the easier path, there will be competitors who will take your clients and your livelihood by being more focused than and outperforming you. Decide how you want to be perceived and strive to make your goal into a reality.

Chapter FOUR

The People

The keys to assembling a winning team and to keeping them happy.

Vital Secret #6

Hire people whose skills complement yours, rather than mirror them.

Vital Secret #7

Skills can be learned, attitudes cannot.

Make the Most

The Young Thief

There was once a fierce tribe that had successfully taken over most of Central Africa. Its warriors were known as conquering heroes and the chief, Taharka, was well-known for his fierce leadership. As time passed, the tribe swept across Africa, winning more and more battles. Villages began to hear about the tribe before they were attacked, and as Taharka's men arrived, fewer and fewer men attempted to fight them for fear they would die.

Whenever Taharka and his men took over a new tribe, the chief would sit down with all the men of the village and decide where he'd place each one in his army. Late one night, after they had just taken over a tribe, Taharka heard a commotion outside his tent. Moments later, two of his warriors came in holding a scrawny young man who was struggling to break free.

"This little runt was caught trying to steal our horses," one of the soldiers told Taharka.

Taharka instructed the soldiers to leave the young man with him. He spent the next twenty minutes interviewing the pug-faced youth and asking a lot of questions to learn his true nature. Taharka learned that the boy's name was Nyack, but he also realized that the boy was clearly a scoundrel. Taharka knew that if he let Nyack go, the young thief would surely try to steal from his army again.

After calling in his guards, Taharka said, "You are to be our prisoner, Nyack. You will come with us to our next crusade until I decide what to do with you."

Several days later, Taharka and his men were marching through the desert to their next destination. As they marched through the dry savannah, one of Taharka's guards asked him a question.

"My chief, why are you keeping this useless runt? He's too skinny to carry anything, he can't fight, and he's even ugly to look at. Why do we need him around?"

Taharka laughed. "That's why I'm the chief and you're not," he told his guard. "Don't be concerned. Everyone has a talent, and I'm sure we'll find this young man's, too."

The tribe continued marching, and by the afternoon, many soldiers had run out of water. Taharka and his men had been unable to find any water throughout the day, and it became clear that water was needed. After thinking for a moment, Taharka had the young thief brought to him.

"Nyack, you are to go off with one of my soldiers and find water," he said. "If you do not succeed, he will chop your limbs off, one by one." Frightened for his life, Nyack immediately turned and ran into the desert, the warrior at his side.

A few hours later, Nyack and the warrior returned with good news. Nyack had found a clean watering hole with plenty of shade. After congratulating him, Taharka had the boy return to his place with the troops.

"I don't understand, my chief," said the warrior who accompanied Nyack on his search. "How did you know he would find water?"

"Well," Taharka responded, "the boy might be a thief, but every person has a talent. I realized from my talk with Nyack that our little friend is resourceful and that he'd do anything to survive. I knew in this situation he'd do the same."

The moral of the story: Find each person's genius and make it work for you.

Putting together a team of people is a fascinating process. Every person hired will bring individual talents and specific weaknesses to your company. The ability to understand both of these aspects and create a harmonized team based on these aspects is one of the essential skills entrepreneurs must master if they intend to create a winning company.

Every successful entrepreneur I have ever known has credited his or her business's success to the people assembled, and to the way that group functioned as a team. However, in the process of growing a company, many common mistakes are made when hiring, regardless of the industry or type of business.

The following two secrets will help you hire the right people and to identify the kind of employees that will make the biggest impact on your business.

■■■■

Vital Secret #6

Hire people whose skills complement yours, rather than mirror them.

Mike founded Jetech Data Systems with his brother at the age of twenty. During the 90s, Mike's company created a standard platform for workforce management software that could be rolled out to large corporations easily and quickly. While the company grew and evolved into the Internet company eLabor, Mike's CFO brought to the company a high degree of confidence and attention to detail.

"We hired a CFO who had a very successful track record, but he needed strong leadership," Mike explained. "He knew accounting, financial mathematics, and analysis so well that I no longer had to worry about these areas. I was determined to find someone for the position who was exacting and detail-oriented, and this particular guy was."

Mike went on to explain how the CFO shouldered some of Mike's workload. "I'm the kind of person who glosses over a contract, or may not even read it, until the final version hits my desk. I simply didn't have the time for that. But my CFO was someone who thoroughly enjoyed reading every word on every page of a contract or document. This meant that the CFO could keep me informed and track changes to documents and contracts."

In fact, Mike even made sure that his top executives complemented each other. "My CFO was great, but he was a numbers person," he explained. "Everything was bottom-line math. But in order to make sure that we also considered the human impact of decisions, we made the Vice President of Human Resources an executive-level position. That person kept my team informed about the morale of the company, in what employees were thinking and concerned about. It was really about addressing the issues of the busi-

ness from a human side. And that kind of perception gave balance to a CFO who was looking at a spreadsheet and crunching numbers."

"At heart, I'm a motivator and salesman," said Mike. "A big-picture guy. But this CFO, as well as the rest of my team, all had skill sets that were very different from mine. I didn't have anyone reporting to me who was a 'yes' person. Absolutely none. And that made a difference in my business."

■■■■

What Vital Secret #6 Should Mean to You

It's often said that great marriages are made of two people with similar values but opposite personalities. I have found that adage to be true in my own life, and a similar idea can be applied to the management teams of successful companies. The more balanced the team, the better prepared your company will be as it faces challenges. Most people are drawn to others who act and think like they do. Yet in order to maintain a well-balanced perspective on issues, it helps to see things in different ways.

The most common conflict found in every organization is that between a sales-type person and an operational-type person. Both are crucial to a business and play a role in its success, but they can seem almost opposite at times. To better understand the differences between these two types of individuals, let's discuss each in detail.

The Sales-Type Personality

This kind of person is led by his heart and ruled by passion. Consider *The Odd Couple* with Oscar, the sportswriter (played by Walter Matthau on screen and Jack Klugman in the TV show) Oscar says what he thinks, wears his heart on his sleeve, and cares passionately about what he believes. These individuals literally scream for their beliefs and are willing to rock the boat if they have to. Things are usually black and white to sales-type personalities, and they can move mountains with their will. They're also accustomed to saying what no one else will, and can get annoyed by calm and deliberate responses.

The Positives

Typical sales-type personalities share certain traits that are important to your company. They can be passionate, gregarious, action-oriented, confident, candid and vocal.

The Challenges

If left unchecked, some sales types can be impatient, arrogant, outspoken and inconsiderate.

The Operational–type Personality

This kind of person is led by his or her brain and ruled by logic. They are introverted by nature. In *The Odd Couple*, think of the Felix character, the conservative businessman (played by Jack Lemon in the movie and Tony Randall in the TV show). Felix is calm and deliberate, tries to stay in control of his emotions, and rationalizes his actions. These people are considerate of other's feelings because they don't want to impose themselves on other people. Operational personalities are able to objectively see other people's perspectives. They are often well organized and thoughtful, but they may look down upon passionate and impulsive behavior.

The Positives

Typical operational-type personalities share certain traits that are important to your company. They can be deliberate, calm, well organized, accommodating and considerate.

The Challenges

If unsupervised, some operational types can be too slow to act, cautious, timid and reserved.

Countless movies and TV shows highlight the conflict between an outgoing person and an introvert. From *Laurel and Hardy* to the *Lethal Weapon* movie series, Hollywood has used this conflict as entertainment time and again. And in almost every film based on this conflict, problems are resolved once both individuals realize that they need each other and that the combination of two types makes for a better whole.

Like everyone in the world, you no doubt have a predetermined tilt toward one personality type and are more comfortable with people similar to you. Likewise, it's not unusual for a company run by a sales type of individual to have a management team that consists of sales-type personalities. The same is true about operationally oriented leaders surrounding themselves with operational personalities in management positions.

It is, however, very unusual to find successful companies where a wide range of personalities and opinions is not present. In fact, the most successful businesses in this country usually have a leader whose right-hand person complements his or her skill sets by being totally different. Few examples are better than Microsoft. The combination of the visionary Bill Gates and the practical Steve Ballmer has turned Microsoft into a software powerhouse. Although both share similar core values, they have completely different personalities.

How to Make Vital Secret #6 Work for You

In order to hire people whose skills complement yours, you need to do four things. You need to evaluate yourself, evaluate your team, strive to balance your company, and make the most of your talent.

1. Evaluate yourself.

Socrates is perhaps best remembered for one statement—that his knowledge was limited to one thing, knowing himself. It goes without saying that the better you know yourself, the better leader you will be.

It's very important that you honestly appraise your strengths and weaknesses as a starting point. Doing so will allow you to hire people who bring to the company skills that you do not have. Ask people who you trust to give you five words that describe your strengths. Then ask them for five words that describe your weaknesses. Obviously, you need to be open minded when people share their thoughts with you.

Realizing they might be afraid to tell their boss his weaknesses one executive asked his employees to write down the traits anonymously. This allowed for more candid responses from people who might have been uncomfortable. A second way to evaluate your weaknesses is to consider the inverse of your strengths. For example, someone who is commended for outspokenness is often someone who doesn't listen to others.

One of the most common complaints I heard about myself while at Centurion was my poor organization skills. I was constantly busy, and if left to me, many tasks simply fell through the cracks and didn't get done. Finally, we hired Ailene to help organize the things I had to get done. As you might guess, her presence had an immediate effect. Even my harshest critics complimented my improved ability to stay organized and were shocked by the change. The fact that so many people had never commented on my problem but became very complimentary afterward indicated that this had been a real issue for me. The same will likely be true for you. There are areas that need improvement.

Assemble this list and use it to evaluate yourself. Determine whether you are a sales-type personality or an operational-type personality.

2. Evaluate your team.

Basically, this means learning the strengths and weaknesses of the people you rely on. Take a look at your team as a whole and ask yourself if there is enough of a counterbalance to offset your own personality. If your company is too aggressively shifted toward either personality, it can create significant problems down the road. A company that has too many sales personalities can often suffer from consistency and reliability issues, while one that has too many operational mindsets can suffer from lackluster growth.

Most industries naturally tilt toward one type or another, but adding balance can create real advantages for your company. For example, an accounting firm or engineering practice will consist mostly of operational type employees. But, adding some sales types to this environment can help the company to become more balanced and see things differently. The same is true for an advertising or distribution company where sales types dominate. Adding some operational viewpoint to these businesses will stabilize and round out the company to help it do better over the long-term. When hiring his replacement, Jack Welch, the very successful former chairman of GE, decided to hire Jeff Immelt in part because of his sales personality. Welch felt the company had become a little too operationally focused and wanted to swing the pendulum back with his replacement.

It's important to realize that some employees will inevitably disagree with the suggestions your new employees will make. This is simply because they're bringing new and different viewpoints to your business. For example, if your business decides to switch from having a human answer telephone calls to having an automated menu for callers, you may get complaints from your technology department, who sees the undertaking as a headache. Your new customer service manager, however, may have suggested the change to help improve your service department.

3. Strive to balance your company.

After you've evaluated yourself and your team, you should strive to create balance by finding people who complement and round out the existing personalities in your business. Doing so will take time, and will increase the amount of disagreement in your company, but it will almost certainly improve the end result. When a group with both personalities is in disagreement, the best way to come to a consensus is to find common ground and build on it. Even though people may disagree on issues, start with things everyone agrees can be built upon.

4. Make the most of your team's talent.

A few years ago I was given a great saying: "Feel the salesman's pain and understand the operator's brain." I've found it to be very useful when working with people. It means that if you want to connect with your team and get the most out of them, don't use the same approach with everyone. It would be a lot easier if everyone fell neatly into one of the two categories that we've mentioned, but life is seldom that easy or simple. Still, it is true that people are either ruled by their head or their heart, so speak to the part of a person that rules their actions.

Sales types will respond best to empathy because they thrive on emotional connections. They want to know that you feel their pain, happiness, or any other emotion. The story in the first chapter about my panic attack with the salesman is a perfect example of this.

For operational types, you cannot use this approach. Their main desire is to be heard and understood, because they're more comfortable with logic than emotions. This means you should connect with them on a practical level and that you should strive to understand what they are saying.

At the end of the day, the primary goal is to create balance in your organization. A team that incorporates all possible viewpoints will be less apt to be surprised and more likely to flourish over a long period of time.

■■■■

Vital Secret #7

Skills can be learned, attitudes cannot.

"I would say that attitude is eighty-five percent important, skill is fifteen percent. Wait, let's make it ninety percent to ten percent." Steve was sharing with me what he thought were the most important traits when hiring somebody. "You know, I have a great example that illustrates this for you." We

were in a Chinese restaurant, eating lunch in Brentwood, California a block away from one of his successful dry cleaning stores.

"We acquired a dry cleaner here in town, and one of my favorite parts of this acquisition was that the manager of the store was extremely experienced and knowledgeable. I knew he would make a great addition to the team, and in fact, I thought so highly of him that we even hired a consulting firm to help him transition into our company. I spent a lot of time trying to get him to fit into our culture, but it never worked. The situation got so bad that my other managers thought I had lost perspective, and after he left us I had to go back and rebuild my credibility with my own team. This particular manager was very talented and had a lot of experience, but just couldn't work with our company. I spent eighteen months trying to make things work, but I learned a valuable lesson... You know, maybe attitude is ninety-five percent of the equation."

What Vital Secret #7 Should Mean to You

This rule speaks for itself—do not confuse a great resume with a great employee. It's interesting how many entrepreneurs have hired someone who had all the experience and credentials needed to play a crucial role in the business, but the person never panned out. I've heard of several cases where an owner's belief in a new hire, especially in a senior management position, literally put the company at risk and jeopardized the relationship between the owner and the other managers.

Every company looks for different attitudes, depending on the culture of the business. And the higher and more important the position within a company, the more important the screening and hiring process becomes. Based on my experience and interviews, there are some common traits that most business owners look for:

- **Ability to fit in.** In a small company, everyone is constantly working with each other. Because of this, it's important that a new member to your team be able to work productively with everyone else. This does not mean they need to have any commonality in sex, race, religion, or background. Rather, they need to share common values, not personalities. As an entrepreneur, you need to imagine the prospective employee working with the rest of your team and how that might look and feel.

In the sports world, there are many instances in which a great athlete was added to a team, but couldn't get along with his new teammates or coaches, and a change became necessary. Teams such as Tom Landry's Cowboys or Phil Jackson's Bulls and Lakers find ways of being champions over the long haul because they hire "their kind" of athletes. During the UCLA basketball reign of the seventies, John Wooden wouldn't recruit people who weren't UCLA types. He would bench any player who didn't behave in the UCLA way, and the school won 10 national championships over an 11-year span—something no school has come close to matching. This is true in the corporate world, too, from Home Depot to IBM. Long-term winners hire people with similar values who add to their team in many ways.

If you have an informal work environment, what impact would somebody who is very structured and formal have on the team? Sometimes an entrepreneur wants to change the dynamic of their workforce, yet making such a change only works if the person shares some fundamental similarities with the existing team.

- **Entrepreneurial comfort level.** Some of the most talented and well-trained prospective employees you'll encounter were raised in a corporate environment. And despite their intentions, not all of them realize how much things can constantly change in an independent growing company. Others may not realize that they won't like the pace or work-style of entrepreneurial enterprises. Because candidates may not understand these differences, it's important to weed out those who are not adaptable enough to work for a small company.

   Imagine that you owned a twenty-five person manufacturing company and were bringing in a manager accustomed to overseeing two hundred people and having an assistant. Would this person be able to function on such a different scale? Could they work with smaller budgets and make do without the bells and whistles they might be accustomed to? Many people in these situations can make the adjustment and lift the quality of a whole organization. Others, however, cannot.

- **I'll do anything mindset.** One of the key traits of any employee who succeeds in an independent business is a willingness to do anything. They typically do not have a mindset of entitlement, and are vertically experienced.

   This means you probably shouldn't hire people who think certain tasks are beneath them. Nor should you hire someone who doesn't know how to do what his employees do. For example, the head of marketing at a small company might have to write copy or lay out a brochure at times. This would seldom occur at a large corporation. Since you probably do not have a lot of backups for various positions, your managers should feel comfortable and be willing to work with the troops when necessary.

How to Make Vital Secret #7 Work for You

In order to find employees who have the attitude you need and can learn the necessary skills, you'll need to do three things. You need to write down an employee type, establish a hiring process, and spend time integrating.

1. **Write down an employee type.**

   First, assemble a list of the attitudes and values you desire in an employee. Consider taking the list of values you assembled in the second chapter and adding those you feel are necessary components for an employee to be happy and welcomed by their peers. A good way to gauge this is to look at your happiest employees and identify what traits make them a "good fit" with your company. Once you have a short list of characteristics, place a mark by those you consider to be "must-haves."

Avoid compromising on those things that are crucial, or you will be doing the candidate and your firm an injustice.

2. Establish a hiring process.

Of course, you will not always be doing all the hiring if your company grows. Therefore, try to develop a consistent methodology that others can follow in the future. The benefit of this is that when one of your employees is in charge of hiring, they'll have a time-tested roadmap to follow. As you develop this methodology, identify how many interviews you'll conduct, what will happen at each one, what questions you'll ask, and what traits you're looking for. Creating a process and perfecting it can make the job a lot easier for whoever follows you in hiring people.

Make a point of meeting several candidates for a position and don't hire anyone after just the first interview. People can change a lot with the second or third visit. Also, try to have an ideal candidate in mind when you start the process, so you can compare candidates to that ideal. A simple methodology is to use a three-step process:

- **Introductory interview.** Find out about the person, why he or she is looking for a new job, what he or she would like to accomplish, and what his or her strengths and weaknesses are. Make notes during the interview about what you like and don't like about the candidate. The first interview is not only a time for you to evaluate the candidate, but he or she will also be evaluating your company. Use this opportunity to get good candidates excited about your company, and rate them on a scale (A, B, C, D, and F) immediately after the interview. If they have a reasonable chance of being hired, give them information about your company prior to the second interview.

- **Follow up interview.** Find out how much they have learned about your industry or your company since the first interview. If the meeting goes well, they should meet their potential fellow co-workers as applicable. Afterwards, get feedback from employees who met with the candidate. Try to ask every employee the same questions about the candidate, so that over time they will know what to expect. Most of the entrepreneurs I spoke with include the candidate's potential work partners in the hiring process. This is called a 360 review and has two major benefits: It empowers your employees and increases the initial productivity of the candidate if you hire them.

- **The closing interview.** Reassess your decision and make the job offer, presuming the person is the right candidate.

  The process you establish can change with time, but most entrepreneurs suggest a hiring process that includes several contacts with the candidate over a period of time. For higher-level management positions, you should consider hosting dinner or lunch, and include the candidate's peers, as this can be quite helpful in accelerating the team building process.

3. Spend time integrating.

Once you have gone through all this work to find the right candidate, make sure you make the most of it. You should have a process of training new employees which will first let them know about the company, then explain job specifics. Throughout this process, the more people the new employee meets, the more productive they will be.

Those entrepreneurs who hire candidates who can do the job well, but also bring other intangible benefits to the company, improve the value of their business with each person they hire.

■■■■■

Taharka knew that the young thief had learned how to survive in difficult situations, and when his men were faced with a survival situation of their own, he called on Nyack's skills to help them.

Find each person's genius and make it work for you.

Take the time to learn everyone's talents and get a complete viewpoint on any issue. Every one of your employees can make a significant contribution to your business, if you make the most of their differences.

Chapter FIVE

The Operations

What to strive for in the day-to-day operations of your company.

Vital Secret #8

Develop procedures that provide consistency and predictability.

The Importance of Sameness

The Great Banana Competition

There once was a town in Africa that cherished bananas, and in that town there were two banana merchants named Masamba and Lobengula. Both had inherited their stores from their parents, and both prided themselves on the quality of their bananas. Their stores were across the street from each other, and each spent much of their day looking across the road to see how the other's business was doing.

Masamba sent his workers out to find only the sweetest bananas. After they spent days searching for the most succulent bananas, by touch alone Masamba would take the best his workers found and put them in his store. Masamba's bananas were a perfect combination of sweetness and firmness, and although every single one tasted wonderful, their appearance varied. His bananas came in all shapes and sizes, and in various shades of yellow, but they always tasted wonderful.

Lobengula, on the other hand, sent his workers out to find only the most beautiful bananas. After they spent days searching for the largest and most beautiful yellow bananas they could find, Lobengula would go through and pick only those whose appearance made his mouth water. Although all the bananas in his store looked delicious, they were not always very sweet, and sometimes they were pasty.

One time, the chief of the local ruling tribe gave birth to his first child, and a huge festival was called for. In order to celebrate, the chief agreed to feed everyone in his rather large tribe only the finest foods for one week. The centerpiece of this festival, he insisted, would be bananas. As the chief prepared for the feast, he sent his most trusted counselor into town to get provisions. As news spread of the feast and the chief's request for bananas, the two merchants wondered who would be chosen to provide the bananas for such a great festival.

The counselor knew the chief had exacting standards, and that he would face dire consequences if the chief was disappointed in any way. When the counselor visited Masamba, he took his time and selected several bananas of varying size and color, then bit into each and every one. Eventually, he looked up at Masamba and said, "These are indeed the sweetest bananas I have ever tasted. Every bite is a pleasure."

He then crossed the street, and his eyes were dazzled by the size and brightness of the bananas in Lobengula's shop. The counselor dug into the piles of bananas and pulled out one after another. "I am amazed at how delicious these bananas look," he told Lobengula. "This is a big decision and it will indeed be a tough choice."

The next day, Masamba received the notice that his bananas would be used in the feast. As he looked across the street to see how his old rival was taking the bad news, he caught sight of a nodding Lobengula. They locked eyes and exchanged glowing smiles.

The counselor had decided to use Lobengula's bananas for the feast's presentations and Masamba's for cooking in the cakes and desserts.

The moral of the story: Be consistent in some way.

The face of a watch tells us what time it is, but it's the machinery behind the face that actually does the work. That too is the case with almost every business. The face of a business is its front office, where the client spends most of his or her time interacting. Yet it's the operations, or the crucial work that occurs in the background, that keep everything functioning.

These operations, which are often called the "back-office" in service companies and "production" in manufacturing companies, are crucial to the success of every business. When it comes to operations, things either work smoothly, or else they create incredible friction in the business. Because operations are usually taken for granted, this is often the least appreciated and over-looked part of a business until things go wrong. And not surprisingly, once that happens there can be an amazing amount of tension between the front office of a business, in other words the sales and service people, and its operations team.

For many businesses, operations only receive serious scrutiny when the company is first established. If it occurs again, it's only because things aren't working as they should later in the life of the business. Usually, problems that arise in operations can be prevented, and many times there are people who try to warn the company of impending risks, but are ignored until something goes wrong.

Imagine that you own a traditional wind-up watch. If it stops ticking once in a while, your first reaction will likely be to shake it. Sometimes that's enough to get it to work again. However, it's usually a signal that something is seriously wrong with the watch and that it should be looked at and repaired. Many people will simply keep shaking the watch until it finally stops ticking altogether.

We've all been there, whether it be a bad TV picture or a rattle in our car. For most of us, a tug here and there or a quick fix might be okay for a while. Unfortunately, many entrepreneurs use similar thinking with their companies. They rely on temporary quick-fix solutions to continue solving the problem. Sometimes this is enough, but this only works until a greater problem comes along that requires serious correction.

But one key difference between a watch and a business is that while it's okay for your watch to be temporarily removed while it gets fixed, it's seldom okay for your company to close a machine or process down while an operational structure gets fixed. That is why it's essential to take pre-emptive measures to make certain that your operations are consistently running smoothly and that you guarantee the company operates in a reliable fashion.

By taking your watch in for cleaning and service, just as most of us do with our cars, you may prevent more serious problems in the future. This is the one area where large corporations usually do better than small businesses because they have established protocols and procedures to ensure consistency. In order to succeed over time you'll need to do the same.

■■■■

Vital Secret #8

Develop systems that provide consistency and predictability.

"They were clients who'd been with us for fourteen years, and one day the wife came in to complain about some buttons being broken." Steve was talking about some clients at his flagship dry cleaning store. *"She had obviously been having a bad day, and insisted that she couldn't possibly ever come back because we had broken two buttons on her husband's shirt. We'd been laundering several of her family's shirts every week for fourteen years. That's hundreds and hundreds of shirts and countless buttons washed every year without incident, and she's ready to stop being a customer because of two broken buttons."*

I asked what he did next. *"What choice did we have? They were valuable clients, so we did what we had to in order to keep them happy, but the frustrating part is from that day on, she looked for things to go wrong. That's what's tough about operational breakdowns. They make your customers lose confidence in you, and it takes a long time to earn that back. It'll be years before this woman gets to the point that she knows everything is fine with her clothes and stops checking for mistakes."*

■■■■

What Vital Secret #8 Should Mean to You

The main reason your business should strive for consistency and predictability is so your clients will know what to expect when they pay for your product or service. Doing so will allow clients to rely on you, which is what all customers want from every business. Whenever people hand over their hard-earned money to a business, they expect a level of reliability that comes from the delivering of goods or services the same way every time. There's no better example of this than McDonalds. No matter where in the world you go, your Big Mac will be cooked the same, taste the same, and look the same, as will all their products. This type of consistency has been the cornerstone of every major brand developed over the past fifty years. It has also been one of the most focused-upon areas of management over the past several decades. Motorola's development of six sigma quality management and its implementation of it into a broad range of the world's largest corporations is testament to this.

As a consumer, can you think of any successful brand that doesn't provide predictable products? Think of several products—soap, cars, food, computers, clothing, car rental—anything. It's next to impossible to come up with one. Now, what if you purchased your regular toothpaste but it tasted different, or your favorite soap suddenly didn't lather as well as in the past? As consumers, we equate predictability and consistency with quality, and we've all come to count on certain traits from the products we use.

I should point out that there is a significant difference between working directly with the end user of your product or service and working through intermediaries. An intermediary, or middleman, could be either a retailer who sells your product, or another company that uses your product or service as part of their own product or service. For example, a bakery might have a storefront and sell their goods directly to customers. But that same bakery could also sell their bread through intermediaries, such as a supermarket that sells the bread to customers, or a hamburger chain that uses their rolls when making hamburgers.

When you sell your product to the end customer, they'll expect a predictable product. But in the rare case it isn't, you'll be able to interact with the customer and try to resolve the problem. For example, in the bakery illustration, let's imagine that some baked goods were left in a humid environment, and as a result, became stale. If a client bought the stale bread directly from the bakery, the baker could rectify the situation by giving the customer a new loaf, and perhaps a free piece of pie as an apology. But if the customer bought the stale bread from an intermediary such as a supermarket, they'll simply return the bread to the store and get their money back without the baker getting an opportunity to fix the situation. In fact, that dissatisfied customer may never buy that bread again. If the stale bread went to a hamburger chain, you'd have a much tougher problem, since the chain wouldn't be able to sell hamburgers with your bread. Worse yet, they might sell their burgers with your stale bread, causing them to lose clients and damaging your business with the chain.

This is why there is even more pressure to create consistent and predictable products when you sell goods and services to other companies. In the end, not only are their orders typically bigger, but a company that buys from you is entrusting your product with their reputation.

To better understand what consistency and predictability means let's take a look at these ideas in both the service industry and the manufacturing industry.

1. The service industry.

A great example of the importance of consistency and predictability for service businesses is the lodging industry. In essence, whenever we choose a hotel, we're paying for a bed to sleep in and a bathroom to use. And depending on our needs and expectations, we might pay as little as $40, or as much as $500 for a room with practically the same location. Yet the difference between these rooms is service, and just as importantly, the predictability and reputation of that service.

Hotel chains like the Ritz Carlton make every one of their hotels look and feel the same, whether they are in Hawaii or Chicago. By comparison, the Four Seasons changes the appearance of their hotels depending on its location, yet their level of service is always the same, as are the beds, sheets, and comforters. Even among the less glamorous hotel chains, those with the most success have similar standards across the board.

Of course, all hotels must provide value for money, but clients of Hilton Hotels also expect their experience at the Hilton in San Francisco to be similar to the Hilton in Sioux Falls. As hotel rooms become cheaper, our expectations for quality service and predictability drop. But regardless of cost, customers are still driven to hotels that provide consistency.

The level of consistency at a service company can be tracked by both tangible and intangible factors, and is evident from both:

Tangible Factors

These are the real items that customers can touch and feel. For hotels, this means things such as the beds and sheets, the soaps and food, and less obvious factors like the gym, pool, and common areas. Even though these factors are usually industry specific, your business should try to provide a consistent level of quality to all tangible aspects. For example, the quality of the bed linens in a hotel should be similar to its towels.

Intangible Factors

These are times when customers interact with your company. For hotels, this can cover everything from check-in and the way room service behaves, to how quickly customers can check out and how employees interact with customers.

These two kinds of factors exist in every service business, whether it's a plumber or an advertising agency. The tangible product is whatever the client is left with after they have paid. For plumbers, this could be new pipes, and for an ad agency it could be a marketing campaign. But the difference in price for these products is often decided by how they are provided.

Of course, at the end of the day, it's just a hotel room with a bed. But as we all know, many people are willing to pay extra for additional perks that come with the room. It's easy to imagine why you'd get frustrated if you paid $500 for a room and didn't get treated in the way you expect.

Airlines are another good example of a service industry. Southwest is a discount airline that makes no bones about moving people like freight, yet their client satisfaction rates are consistently among the highest in the industry. This is simply because people know what they are paying for, and they get it again and again. In comparison, full service airlines keep changing. Sometimes there's food on a flight, and sometimes there isn't. One day you may pay $100 for a particular flight, and a month later you're charged ten times that amount for the same flight. Such inconsistency costs the full service airlines a fortune in dissatisfaction. Of course, when they hit tough times, these airlines have no problem finding money from large institutions. Your business, sadly, will not have friends with such deep pockets.

If your company is in the service business, it's important that you identify what level of service you intend to provide, charge appropriately for that service, and deliver that service the same way over and over again.

2. The manufacturing industry.

When it comes to manufacturing products, customers want to know that what they are buying will always be the same. Just as important, customers are willing to pay a premium for consistency because they understand the cost of buying faulty goods. Two great examples of this lie in the microchip making industry and the bakery business. Since both these industries create goods that are used in end products, there is excruciating and intense pressure from customers for consistency. Fortunately, manufacturing has improved by leaps and bounds, thanks to quality controls like six sigma (which measures the amount of defects in products and services) that have been implemented over the past several years. Most companies use these quality control systems, and they help to reduce faults and variability on products being manufactured.

In a manufacturing company, both tangible and intangible factors need to be consistent, but with a different focus than a service company.

Tangible Factors

This refers to the product the customer is buying. If your product is sold to another company, they will probably have very exacting standards of quality. Microchips are used in all kinds of products ranging from computers to cameras to cars. A faulty chip means the customer's end product will be faulty as well; therefore customers often insist on established default parameters, such as the amount of faulty chips they are willing to accept per shipment. In fact, these parameters exist even when the product is sold directly to individuals, but through an intermediary such as a department store or other retailer.

If your product is sold directly to the public and the end user is your customer, he or she will also have expectations regarding the reliability of the product. But if it isn't, you will have an opportunity to correct the situation directly, since you're also servicing your product.

Intangible factors

This refers to interactions the customer has with your company. For many manufacturers, there is no interaction with the end user of the product. The majority of interaction is with other companies who buy their product. As a consequence, there is much more pressure for these manufacturing companies to be accessible and address issues as they arise. The way these businesses deal with ongoing issues such as returns and payment delays needs to be consistent. For example, Dell is known for its customized computers, as well as personalized support at every level.

If these companies behave differently in similar or repeated situations, they inevitably lose credibility as a serious supplier. This occurs because many larger companies expect them to have policies and procedures for every aspect of their business.

How to make Vital Secret #8 work for you

You need to do four things in order to develop procedures that provide consistency and predictability. You need to evaluate your company and the industry, evaluate your client, measure your predictability and consistency, and improve your operating procedures.

1. Evaluate your company and the industry.
   Begin by addressing the following questions:

   - Is your business primarily a service company or a product company?

- How consistent and reliable are you in both the tangible and intangible aspects of your business?

- How does your business's pricing compare to others? In other words, are you a high-end provider or a low cost provider?

- What percentage of your clientele are repeat customers?

- How reliable and predictable is your industry in general, and how reliable is your business compared to others in the industry?

It's important that you answer these questions honestly, because by doing so, you can understand where your company currently exists in terms of quality and reliability in your industry. Write down your answers to these questions and also have your employees and peers answer them. See if they have similar perceptions of your company.

For example, the seventies were known as the dark period of the United States car market because American cars at the time were considered unreliable gas-guzzlers. The Japanese were accustomed to making economical cars that were very reliable, and when Japanese cars were first available in the United States, their quality and reliability standards were so superior to American cars that they captured a huge share of the U.S. market until American carmakers improved their quality standards to compete.

2. Evaluate your client.

Follow up by asking the following questions:

- Who do you sell your product/service to?

- Are your clients other businesses or the public? If you work with both, remember that each has different priorities and goals.

- What are the three most important things clients expect when buying your product or service?

- How well do you consistently meet your clients' needs?

In order to maintain good relationships with all your clients, their experiences with your company should be stable and consistent. Ask existing clients how predictable and consistent they view your company to be. Find out what the most reliable aspect of your company is, as well as what areas they consider to be less reliable.

3. Measure your predictability and consistency.

Basically, any form of quality control measures a company's error rate and improves it. Of course, it's easier to measure tangible aspects than intangible ones.

For example, if you're a baker, it's easy to sample every few loaves to ensure that there are no quality shortfalls. But when it comes to the intangible aspects of a business, creativity is necessary to create measuring standards. One way might be to have an ongoing sample survey, or to log calls of customer complaints. Often a spike in call volume warns that something has happened, be it good or bad.

One company surveyed different clients once a quarter by mailing them a simple return postcard. It asked them to score the company on a scale of one to five regarding the reliability of a few aspects of their business. When the responses began to drift, the company knew something was going wrong. They also logged calls and counted what percentage of the daily calls resulted from service issues. All of these things help to identify when a business is slipping. The best gauge though is returning customers; if fewer people come back it is a sign that you are doing a bad job setting client expectations, you are not as reliable as you used to be, or one of your competitors has moved ahead of you in meeting the client's needs.

4. Improve your operating procedures.

Things are often done in a certain way simply because that's the way they've always been done. Yet there is always a possibility that improvements in technology or personnel might make the existing procedures obsolete. Because of this, you should try to take the time once in a while to ask how things can be improved. Ask how certain operational functions would be done today if you were starting over from scratch, because that's how improvements happen over time—one at a time, step by step.

Remember that even if you do not make the effort to re-evaluate your procedures, your competitors will. It's always easier to be in the lead than be forced to play catch up. Lexus has a great slogan that speaks to the process of improving; "one thousand small improvements." Cars are always getting better, that is also certainly true in your industry though it might not be as visible as it is in a car. So try to continually make improvements that help your company be reliable, because the more reliable you are, the more successful you will be getting and keeping clients.

■■■■

The great banana competition ended with an unusual twist. Both merchants were successful because even though they had different strengths, each showed consistency and quality in their respective strengths.

Be consistent in some way.

This is true in everyday business too. Having a reputation for reliability will help you thrive in all environments.

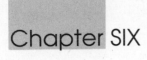

Chapter SIX

The Product

The secret of creating a successful product or service and

getting a premium price for what you do.

Vital Secret #9

Provide differentiated products and services;
you cannot win the low cost battle.

Be Different

The Gold Rush

On the outskirts of a small town in Southern Africa, in the midst of gold rush fever, lived an incredibly successful merchant. He had a huge store with all the supplies any prospector could need. Every day new prospectors would come to town from all parts of Europe after enduring a long boat ride and a treacherous trek from the coast to the gold-rich hills in Kimberley. They would arrive in town with their life's savings, and all of their accumulated life's possessions, hoping to strike it rich. The exhausted travelers would come into the merchant's emporium to buy their supplies for the mining days ahead. Though his pricing was high at times, the merchant prospered as word of the gold strikes from the surrounding mountains spread and more and more people visited his huge and growing emporium. Whenever people ran out of money chasing their dreams, they were promptly replaced by others coming to chase their own dreams of wealth.

Sometimes a new store would attempt to compete with the merchant. When this happened, the merchant simply offered huge discounts on whatever products his competitors sold, and eventually the other store was driven out of business. Afterwards, the merchant always increased his prices to make up for lost profits.

One day, a failed miner opened a new store across the street from the emporium. It was a small store with few goods, so the merchant ignored it. After all, only the poorest miners were going to shop there, and the merchant knew that the miners who went across the street were always out of money. He had seen many competitors in the past and this was one of the weakest attempts he'd ever seen. However as the months passed, the store began to grow. The powerful merchant dropped his prices to ensure the demise of this new competition. This time, though, the store across the street did not promptly disappear. In fact, it continued to grow. Sometimes there was even a line outside the store. Soon the merchant cut prices even further, but he continued losing customers to the pest across the street.

One day at the local saloon, the wealthy merchant walked over to his competitor and asked, "How is it possible? I keep cutting prices and you still have a flood of people lining up outside your store. How much longer are you willing to keep losing money?"

The former miner smiled and said "As long as there are miners who've spent all their money with you."

So the next day, the merchant took a closer look at the line outside the store across the street and noticed that everyone was holding something. Some were holding clocks, others tents and sleeping bags, others large trunks.

Instead of selling goods for cash, the store across the street was letting miners trade their valuables for everyday supplies. The owner then sold the valuables for a handsome profit.

The moral of the story: Be unique in solving problems and you will be handsomely rewarded.

■■■■

In a capitalistic society, where entrepreneurship and business competition are a part of life, understanding how to compete is the cornerstone of success. The products and services you offer to clients are a crucial element that will determine your ability to survive in a marketplace that quickly adapts to new developments.

While there is a distinct difference between a product and a service, there are also shared traits among both. Simply put, a product is a tangible item or object, such as a brick or a bicycle that is sold to a client, while a service usually refers to an action that a client pays for, such as a hair cut or accounting services. However, most items that a customer pays for include elements of both. After all, even the brick merchant has to take the call, deliver the order, and do billing, all of which impact the customer. For the purpose of this book, the term product will be used to define both products and services and will include anything for which a consumer is willing to pay.

In the previous chapter, we discussed the need for predictability and consistency in operations. Building on those lessons, it goes without saying that your product also needs to be delivered in a consistent and predictable manner. The ideas discussed in the chapter about operations should be applied to your products as well as your operations, since you want to offer products that are highly valuable and will adapt to changes in the marketplace. However, if they are not predictable and consistent, people won't return to your business.

Choices, Choices

No matter what kind of product is being built, every entrepreneur must decide how to stand out from his competition. Few business owners realize the importance of this choice, but one of the keys to success lies in how a business decides to develop and deliver its products to its customers.

While the possibilities may seem limitless, there are really only two options available to every business. One option is to become the low-cost provider, while the other is to offer a differentiated product. Simply put, is your product going to be the cheapest out there, or is it going to be different from your competitor's? This concept can be illustrated in a product as basic as table salt. Competitors could try to be as cheap as possible, by spending little money on packaging or marketing, or they could choose to create a valuable brand, as Morton's has done in the salt market. Though the products are all identical, Morton's can command a premium price because it is a known brand and is perceived to be of higher quality.

As a business owner, you need to find ways to differentiate your product from the competition. This includes being aware of everything that your product could become, and which aspects of it your clients are willing to pay for. Let's consider a couple of examples.

First, let's look at an example in the hard product industry. If you were developing a brand of toothpaste, what could make it stand out from other toothpastes in the grocery store? Well, it's obvious that people expect it to be consistent and predictable; in other words, every time they squeeze the tube, they are going to get the same product. The other consideration when creating a product like toothpaste is what else it is going to do. Is it going to have whitening agents? Is it going to have tartar control? Are the packaging and flavor going to be geared toward children or adults? Any of these choices would differentiate the toothpaste from competitors. Issues as subtle as the color and the lettering you use, or the stores that you choose to sell your product through, tell customers something about your product. For example, Tom's Toothpaste is created for environmentally conscious people, while Rembrandt Toothpaste is known for its teeth-whitening agents.

For the service industry, let's consider a hair salon. If you own a hair salon, you need to decide how you'll stand out from the competition in your area. Are you going to be more convenient than other salons? Perhaps you'll be faster than your competitors. Do you want to be known as a high service salon that offers luxury to clients? Do you want to be on the cutting edge of trends and styles? You have to determine what you're going to offer that will make clients come to you. One example of this is Supercuts, a national chain that strives to be the cheapest and fastest place to get haircuts anywhere in the country.

As you can see, there is a wide range of alternatives to choose from when you are building a product. As an entrepreneur with limited resources, however, the most important thing to understand is which of these available options your clients are willing to pay the most for and therefore provide the highest potential for reward.

When building your product, you can have strong opinions about how it needs to be built, but in doing so, you need a good understanding of what the marketplace needs, wants, and is willing to pay for. And as you consider your options, remember that no decision can be made in a vacuum.

■■■■

Vital Secret #9

*Provide differentiated products and services;
you cannot win the low cost battle.*

A great example of differentiation comes from Kevin, one of the builders of one of the nation's largest golf course management companies. The company operated golf courses and country clubs, and grew from 17 locations in the early '80s to over 300 by the new millennium.

"You know," Kevin told me, "golf courses each have their own individual personality. It's not like fast food or chain stores, where you strive to provide the same look, feel, and experience at each location. So we really had to look at each course as its own individual entity. The way we were able to remain attractive and compete with other courses was to make sure we provided the best value around."

"If you play golf," Kevin explained, "municipal golf courses, which are usually run by a city or county, are most always the cheapest places to play. Yet these courses are also usually in [the] worst shape of any around. So we looked to compete with those courses in terms of price, but provide a much better course for the money. We wanted people to come in, pay a twenty-five or thirty dollar green fee for a round of golf, but leave thinking that the service and quality of the course was just as good as one that might cost fifty or sixty dollars to play."

This approach not only differentiated Kevin's business, but also allowed it to grow vastly in the '70s and '80s. *"We got so good at improving courses and making them heads above the rest, that we were seeing as many as thirty thousand more golfers a year on our courses than our competitors."*

Another way the company differentiated itself was by creating something unheard of for a public golf course at the time: a reservation center. *"We created a call center to handle reservations for our courses,"* Kevin told me. *"As you can imagine the nine o'clock and ten o'clock a.m. spots on a Saturday fill up pretty fast, so instead of losing those golfers to a competiting course, we realized that if we could tie all the reservations for our courses together, we could suggest other courses of our own that had that time available."*

Once implemented, this meant that golfers who called up seeking reservations for a particular course at a certain time were offered the same tee time at a nearby course if their first selection was unavailable. *"We were really able to leverage our demand and spread golfers out, while still keeping them as customers. It worked out really well since people knew that they were calling a center with multiple courses, we were often the first call they made."*

■■■■

What Vital Secret #9 Should Mean to You

As we discussed, there are two choices every entrepreneur faces when building a product. The first is to be price focused, while the second is to offer a differentiated product. Yet once you decide, you can't ignore the other alternative completely. You'll still have to be sensitive to how your product is different, or how your price compares to the market.

The problem for many entrepreneurs is that they go into business assuming that because they're new, they need to charge as little as possible in order to compete. In doing so, they fail to realize that although it's easy to lower their prices, it's very tough to raise them, especially if they start up with low prices. As the secret indicates, you can never be the lowest-cost provider. Why? Because unless you are in a small, clearly defined niche requiring unique knowledge (which makes you differentiated anyway), there will always be a bigger, better-resourced company that can outsource production and use its size to squeeze suppliers. There will always be a bigger company with a cheaper cost of capital that can come and steal your market once it appeals to them if you differentiate by price alone. Because of this, you should not rely on price alone to separate yourself from the pack. Using a simple example, let's look at what happens if you decide on this choice. Let's imagine that you want to open a hair salon: Hair Salon X, (we will come up with a better name later, one that suits our positioning).

You decide to start with a very simple premise; "When I open, I'm going to charge less for a haircut than anyone else, and that'll get people to come to my salon." Once you open, customers start booking appointments, excited by your low prices. This continues for two or three months, until other salons in the area drop their prices lower than yours. You realize that you can't lower your prices any further without losing money, and your customers, who are all price focused (because that's how you attracted them) start going to other salons. Since you're not offering any unique service other than low price, your customers see no reason why they should stick around. You are desperate for business, but there's nothing you can do.

As you can see, this is not a good way to start a business. Since you don't have an established customer base, having very low prices as soon as your business opens puts you at a huge competitive disadvantage. Your competitors can immediately match your prices, and because of their established customer base and already established income, can survive in a way you can't unless you have enough capital to wait them out, even then you'd have a weak business position. As illustrated by the story at the beginning of the chapter, unless you have the balance sheet and cash of your competitors, you will need to differentiate your new business in order to survive.

This rule applies to any business, regardless of service or product sold. Most successful businesses have a totally different view about how they build a product. Instead of deciding in a vacuum, they first look to understand what clients need, and then build a product that is profitable at an attractive price (often higher than their competitors). They are usually able to charge more because they are filling a need in the market that no one else has identified, and they are doing it better than anyone else.

As an example of this in the service industry, look at American Express. Not only is it one of the most expensive credit cards in the country, but it charges both vendors and users of the card high fees, far above what anyone pays for a Visa or MasterCard. Yet the card remains popular for one reason: The company provides a much higher level of service than other credit card companies, including concierge services and booking airline tickets for users. It is also branded as a more prestigious card. The result? Fantastic profit margins year after year.

In the production industry, a good example is the Hummer H2 recently launched by General Motors. As a modified version of a military vehicle, the car brings its manufacturer huge profit margins and is successful because GM realized that in these insecure times following 9/11, people would pay a premium to drive a sturdy, almost military-type vehicle. The company listened to its customers, who said they loved the original Hummer because it was industrial and had a military background, but they also wished it were a little more road-friendly (a little smaller) and also quieter and more comfortable. GM built a smaller, more luxurious, and lower-cost version of the Hummer. As a result, the newly created H2 is so popular that customers have to get on waiting lists to buy the car. It's an immensely successful, expensive product with huge profit margins in an already saturated SUV market because GM successfully filled a need that the market had.

Why Define Your Product?

One of the main reasons every company needs to differentiate its product is to have front-of-mind awareness with its consumers. This means being the first company that comes to mind when a specific issue arises. For example, if you live in the western part of the country and need to fly somewhere as cheaply as possible, what name comes to mind? Typically, it is Southwest Airlines. If you want the newest electronic device, such as a TV or camcorder that works really well, is high quality, and has all the latest technology, what name pops into your head? Probably Sony. If you want an expensive, high-end watch that people will recognize, what would you buy? Probably a Rolex.

Almost every product is categorized by consumers at some level, and you either have their front-of-mind awareness, or you don't. This can work in both a general and specific sense, from someone thinking "That company makes the best electronics," all the way down to "When I need to get a great haircut, but want to be pampered as well, that salon is the best place to go."

Consider hotels. When making a reservation for a hotel room, do you want something that's good enough for your needs, or something luxurious with a lot of extras? Before you even make a selection, you already know there's a difference between the Ritz-Carlton and a Holiday Inn. That's because both hotels have clearly established what differentiates them from other hotels, and successfully conveyed that to customers.

How Can You Be Differentiated?

We will examine niche marketing in detail in the next chapter. However when building your product, identifying client needs is crucial. There are several ways your product can be differentiated. Typically this will be incorporated in the features you include in your product.

1. **By geography**. Country, region, city, or neighborhood you will service or sell to. Your product might be more sensitive to the geographic issues faced by your customers, whether it's strictly due

to location or other factors such as weather, culture, or business practices in the region. Being local can be very important in smaller towns. An organic farmer can provide fresher produce to his local town than a large supermarket. Some people would probably be willing to pay extra for that.

2. **By demographics**. Specifics about the person or companies you want to help. For example for direct-to-consumer businesses, what is the income, age, sex, and education level of your ideal client, and what are their specific needs? If you sell to businesses, what size are they, what industry are they in and what are the unique features these clients need?

3. **By unique knowledge**. What do your employees know that others don't? What makes your team special? For example, perhaps you own a tax accounting firm that has former IRS examiners on its staff.

4. **By unique features**. Offering unique ways to solve problems for customers. An example of this is an investment advisor emailing all of a client's statements in an easy to understand format at the end of each week rather than mailing them on paper once a quarter. If you have a product, maybe it's smaller or has unique ingredients.

5. **By culture**. Having a corporate culture that is appealing to customers: for example like the Ritz Carlton formality that runs through every hotel, or by comparison the informality of Southwest airlines. This could also mean being more innovative than anyone else or being more responsive than your competitors. Remember the Avis "We try harder" tag line?

As we've said before, the more specific you are in these areas, the better. You can differentiate yourself by targeting customers in a specific neighborhood within your city. Your demographic could be college educated parents in their forties. You may target doctors, lawyers, or stockbrokers. And you may even want to go after certain groups such as fans of a professional sports team, or alumni of a certain college. As you consider these areas, you'll start to form an idea about whom you're building your product for. Basically, you're beginning to identify your target market. However this is not about marketing—we'll cover that in the next chapter—this is about understanding your client and building a compelling and valuable product.

Let's go back to the hair salon for an illustration. Say you're opening a salon for women, but you want a more specific target market. Geography is very important because people will probably not commute too far for a haircut, so you'll need to be in a convenient location for your customers. You'll also need to identify the size and details of your demographic. How many women live and work in a particular area? How old are they? Do they have children? Consider their professions. What kinds of jobs do they have? Do they work regular business hours? How many of them are college educated?

After asking these questions, let's assume your target market is professional women who have a college education. You may learn that most work downtown and have families, and would enjoy being treated to a relaxing haircut during their lunch break. Based on this information, you'd know the best location to set up your salon and how to attract these women as customers. But most importantly it would help you to define what your salon should look like, what kind of staff you should hire, what features you should offer, what hours you should be open, even what name you should have. Answering these kinds of questions is very important when building or improving your product or service. Instead of simply opening and hoping to be all things to all people, you can be everything to a very specific group, and be well compensated for it.

If you're already in business, then your clients already have a perceived view of where you fit in with the competition and how you differentiate yourself. However, you can still use these questions to refine your product. Instead of determining a target market, you can get this information from existing customers.

There is probably not a product you can come up with that has not already been tried in the past. But there is still almost certainly a combination of features and benefits that will be truly unique. After all Southwest Airlines was basically using people and planes to move humans from one place to another, just like all of their competitors. However the way they put everything together made them unique. Successful businesses are not built on originality, but their ability to deliver a needed product in a unique way. The common theme separating products that survive and thrive from those that don't is the ability to understand the marketplace's needs and the ability to execute better than anyone else on the fulfillment of those needs.

To quote hockey great Wayne Gretzky, when asked why he was able to get to the puck before everyone else, "I skate to where the puck is going to be, not where it is." That mindset should always be in your mind when developing a product or service.

In order to differentiate your product, you need information about your target clients, and the best way to do this is through field research. This simply means identifying what clients need or want by going out and asking them. Surprisingly though, many successful pioneering products are not built this way. This is because people cannot imagine something they would be willing to pay for. When asked in research situations, most individuals say they want to have whatever is already out there at a lower price. Even though this often happens when you do field research, it is very important to understanding what people see as their alternatives.

How to Make Vital Secret #9 Work for You

When building a product, there are three things that need to be accomplished: You need to understand the competitive market; understand the importance of certain features and why they matter; and prioritize and rank those features, so that your product speaks to the market's needs. To better illustrate this process, let's take a look at each step using the hair salon example.

> **1. Understand the competitive market.** This means going out and asking a sample of people in your demographic about simi-

lar services they already own and use. You need to find out what they like about these services and what they expect from them. The number of people you ask is up to you. Reach to the point where you feel very comfortable in your understanding of the market. Obviously the more, the better. Don't get too complex; simply get to the point where you feel knowledgeable about what people want.

In building the hair salon that targets working women, you would go out and ask a sample of working women in your neighborhood about the haircuts they currently get. What do they look for when getting their hair cut? Do they want to relax and chat with their stylist, or do they want to get in and out quickly? How often do they go? What does their salon not provide that they would like to see? Would they like to get their nails done, or have a drink while they wait? When do they get their hair cut? On their lunch break? In the evenings? On weekends? What do they currently pay? These questions give you the information necessary to understand the current market for hair salons.

2. **Understand the importance of each of the features.** Look at the results of your questions to find out what things are the most important to clients and how this impacts their decisions.

After asking these questions about hair salons, you may realize that the majority of women want to take a break from their work lives; that they want to sit down and chat with their stylist, and be able to relax. Based on this, you'd be smart to focus on luxury in your salon. Maybe you'd want to have a café latte waiting for customers and hire hairdressers that are very outgoing and talkative. Your research might also indicate that women want to come in on their lunch break, and be in an out in an hour. This would let you know that late morning to early afternoon would be a busy time for your salon, and that you might need to make sure customers don't have long waits. Maybe you'd want to implement a policy stating that no customer wait more than ten minutes for their stylist. And if the responses indicate that they are willing to pay more for this luxury and speed, then you'll know that you won't have to charge less than other salons.

3. **Prioritize and rank those features, and build your product so that it speaks to the market's needs.** This means taking your list of what is important and determining which features are more important than others. Usually this comes down to sheer statistics and how many people gave a particular response to a question.

Once you know what's important in a hair salon, you need to find out which of these features are the most important to customers. If 60 percent of women you surveyed said they want to relax when they come into a salon, and 85 percent said it's important they get in and out in an hour, you know that it'll be more important to focus on short waiting times and speed than providing customers with something to drink. Although both may be a part of your salon, you'll want to be known for your speed with lunchtime appointments. But by incorporating both these elements, you'll be an attractive option to the majority of your target market.

You may find it difficult to rank these features, because you're concerned about alienating customers. But it's necessary to realize that you're not going to make everyone happy. With the salon, for example, some women are going to want to be done quickly, while others may not want to pay a premium for your speed and luxury. This acknowledgement will help you determine how inclusive of your clients you need to be in order to build a successful business. If there are enough women in the area willing to pay a premium for a fast, luxurious haircut, you won't need to worry about competitors. But if enough women are willing to wait at another salon that is more luxurious, you may need to make luxury a priority over speed.

All three of these goals have one very simple target: to understand your clients' needs right from the beginning, and to build a product that fills the needs of the marketplace.

Like the new store owner, many people tried to compete with the successful merchant. Yet none of them succeeded until someone identified the real service those miners needed. Who better than a former miner? He correctly identified that the ability to dispose of their old goods for additional supplies was really important to them, because they had no cash left.

Providing unique products and services is imperative in competitive markets.

There will always be competitors who are bigger and have a stronger market position than you. However, the size of these businesses prevents them from appealing to all the needs of their clients in every unique space. This is why you need to build a clearly defined product. When you differentiate your product and business, you have your customers' undivided and total attention on a specific area. This will allow you to prosper and grow where others won't. And when that happens, it will be difficult for other businesses to compete with you.

Chapter SEVEN

Sales and Marketing

How to compete with the big boys and win,

and how to decide where you should market.

Vital Secret #10

Identify and market to a niche.

Vital Secret #11

Referrals are the cheapest and most effective way to get clients.

Vital Secret #12

Create a self-sustaining sales system.

Find Your Target

The Beautiful Beads

One beautiful Saturday morning, a young African woman named Christina took her four daughters to the village market. To help support her family, Christina sold beads to shoppers in the village square, and it had come time for her daughters to help her with her work.

First, Christina set up a booth for two of her daughters, Alice and Naja, at one end of the market. Her daughters helped her lay out beads on the table in an appealing manner to attract as many passersby as possible. Once they were finished, Christina took her other two daughters, Ullu and Martha, to the other end of the market to set up their booth. As she helped her children, she gave them each the same advice. "Smile a lot and ask as many people as possible if they want some beads."

As the day progressed, Christina went from one booth to the other to check on her daughters. First, she watched as Alice and Naja did exactly as they were told, going from person to person, beads in hand. Smiling sweetly they would ask "Would you like some beads?" There were so many people walking around that they could barely get to half of the people they saw. Most of the villagers were carrying packages of food or tubs of water, and they would say, "Those are very nice beads, but my hands are full." Chistina counted the beads left on the table, and was happy to see that her daughters had sold 32 strands. She encouraged Alice and Naja to keep asking people and that she'd be back at lunchtime.

Then, Christina went to check on Ullu and Martha. As she arrived at their booth, she watched the two girls approach only certain people, mostly women. She asked her daughters to join her at the table and explained, "You're missing so many great opportunities. You know your sisters Alice and Naja have sold lots of beads because they are asking everyone."

Christina then reached into the first box of beads and began counting the strands to see how poorly they'd done. Once she finished, she asked for the other box.

"It's gone," replied Ullu.

"What do you mean?" Christina asked. "That other box had 200 strands in it."

"We sold them," explained Martha.

"But, girls, you're not even going up to everyone!" Christina said to her daughters.

"But mother," explained Ullu, "we got tired of people telling us that their hands were full, so we decided to only go up to people that had nothing in their hands."

Christina watched her daughters again as they approached empty-handed women who would quickly reach into their pockets and buy whatever strand of beads the girls were holding. Ullu and Martha also approached young girls with the beads, who would then ask their parents to buy them. Christina watched as one parent after another put their packages down to pay while their daughters picked out their favorite strand of beads.

In the next twenty minutes, Ullu and Martha sold the rest of their beads. When they were done, Christina bought her daughters a sweet mango to congratulate them.

The moral of the story: Sales is a numbers game; the more qualified the prospects, the better the numbers.

Sales and marketing are the tools and processes that companies use to get new clients. Many people have a natural love for the selling process, while others tolerate it as a necessary evil. Regardless of your personal opinion, it will be almost impossible for your business to generate new clients without a disciplined sales and marketing program.

In every industry, there are companies who, despite inferior products, consistently have superior financial results because they sell and market their services better than the competition. In fact, if you compare two companies with similar products, the company with better sales and marketing skills will usually charge more, and sell more, than the competitor who doesn't place a priority on sales.

Selling and marketing is important to any company because of one simple word—inertia. Inertia is the universal force that causes people and objects to keep doing what they are already doing. In order to change a person's actions, something has to create a desire strong enough to cause that person to make the change. Yet this is just the first step of the process. You cannot change people's actions and make them new clients without getting them to act, which takes selling.

In its simplest form, selling is nurturing a desire for action in a potential client, and helping them stay focused on that action, in order to shift their inertia toward you to become your customer. There is a key difference between marketing and selling. Marketing creates a desire for something, while selling creates an urge to act on that desire. Working together, these two can be incredibly powerful and overcome any inertia.

For example, let's look at banks. Obviously, your current bank does what you expect it to do: it keeps your money, cashes your checks, and provides other standard services. Assuming that your current bank is meeting your expectations and working fine, why would you want to change banks? Well, let's say something has convinced you that the services you're getting aren't as good as what you'd get from a competing bank, and that you'd be better off with a new bank. If you believed that, you'd seriously consider switching banks. Of course, this would only happen if something or someone was able to convince you that the new bank could provide a better solution and made it important enough and easy enough for you to change. That's where a marketing and sales campaign comes in.

This is the case for almost every shift in relationships we make as customers, and your potential clients are no different. Your prospects not only have limited time, but they're accustomed to what they're already doing. And in order to make any of them a new client, they must be convinced that they'll benefit from working with you. More importantly, they need to be prodded to make that change. Your desire for prospective clients to act must be greater than their desire for things to stay the same.

In this chapter, we'll discuss three vital secrets to successfully generate new clients for your business.

■■■■

Vital Secret #10

Identify and market to a niche.

After spending 10 years in marketing and working in finance, Greg founded his company with his wife Tina. By offering no-load variable annuities, the company quickly became one of the nation's leading insurance marketing services that focuses exclusively on consumers. Thanks to cost-effective lead generation and focusing on a specific niche, Greg sold the business after a successful 15-year run.

"One of the ways we were able to successfully market to niches were through affiliations," Greg explained. "For example, we'd partner with groups such as Good Sam, the national club of recreational vehicle owners, and the Aircraft Owners and Pilots Association, which was an organization of professional pilots as well as hobbyist pilots. Once we partnered with these groups, they gave us their seal of approval and recommended us to members, and in turn, we were able to market to these members and focus on that group's specific needs."

But Greg found niches in other ways. "We also went to financial and investment newsletters, and formed partnerships with them. People like Dick Fabian and companies like Philips Publishing recommended us to their readers, which allowed us to market and advertise to those specific groups as well. At the height of our business, we were appearing and recommended by up to thirty different newsletters."

"There's a few reasons this worked so well for us," he explained. "First, newsletters were in the business of giving advice and recommendations, and as a business, we represented all the leading insurance companies. We were also able to offer annuities nationwide and were easy to contact and work with. So being able to offer products from a variety of companies, and to do so across the country, meant that we could apply our business to different people in different locations."

One of the ways Greg's company was able to identify potential clients was through phone numbers. "We could tell which organization or association a caller would belong to based upon the 800 number they used to contact us. A particular number was used for members of Good Sam, while another number was given to readers of Dick Fabian's newsletter. That in itself gave us a way to begin discussions with clients while recognizing who referred them to us. Once we sent them materials about our products, we mentioned the newsletter or organization that referred them to us, which brought the referral and niche whole circle. Really, the best thing about this kind of affinity marketing was that instead of spending forty-five cents to send a letter to someone we didn't know and who may not be interested, we were spending that forty-five cents to send a letter to someone we did know and who we knew was interested in our products because they were built specially for their market."

▪▪▪▪▪

What Vital Secret #10 Should Mean to You

One of the major mistakes all business people make at some point is believing that they can be all things to all people. Most successful entrepreneurs we spoke to told us how they spread themselves too thin, and as a result, didn't make an impact anywhere. It's important to realize that almost all successful businesses start by marketing to a niche.

A niche is simply a segment of the population. Anyone can be analyzed and categorized through a series of filters, such as age, education, hobbies, location, income, or others. These filters are then used to narrow the focus of a target group almost like a funnel. The process starts with a big group; as more filters are used, the target gets narrower and the group gets smaller.

For example, let's say there are two competing banks: Bigshot Bank, a large multinational bank, and Cowboy Bank, a regional bank based in Denver. Both want Jay to become a client of their bank. Jay is a 42-year-old doctor who lives in Denver. He has his own practice, his wife is an accountant, and they have two children. Based on the following actions, which bank do you think will get Jay's business?

- Jay receives a letter from Bigshot Bank stating that it is a great bank because it is so big, it can help anyone with anything.

- Jay receives three letters from Cowboy Bank stating that it is a great bank for doctors because it understands the complicated needs doctors face, as well as the demands of having a family and ensuring their security and comfort.

All people want to be treated uniquely, and the more specific your company is about the type of clients you're looking for, the more effective you'll be reaching those people. There's a huge advantage to being specific, because it is one thing large corporations cannot do.

As you might expect, a huge bank like Bigshot cannot market specifically to doctors in Denver. This is because Bigshot needs all doctors everywhere, as well as everyone in Denver, as their market. Companies such as Bigshot have huge expenses, and if their target market is not large enough, those clients will not make enough of an impact in their earnings.

A regional bank such as Cowboy, however, can do very well marketing specifically to a group such as doctors living in Denver—presuming the target market is large enough. This is why no matter how big corporations get, there is always room for small businesses that market to a specific niche. In this case, the message Cowboy Bank provides is certainly more specific to Jay's needs.

Second, a regional bank in Denver would get more repeated contact with Jay than a national bank out of New York. This is because Bigshot Bank spends its marketing dollars to entice potential clients all over the world. It has the muscle to sell to lots of people everywhere, but not to specific groups. In contrast, Cowboy Bank can do several mailings to the same person rather than only one mailing.

Let's take a moment to discuss segmenting, or identifying a niche, in more detail. In the example we just used, Jay represents a certain segment of the population because his traits were used as filters. He is a doctor, a male, lives in Denver, 42 years old, married, and has two children. So these six characteristics become filters regarding profession, gender, location, age, marital status, and parental status, respectively. If these filters were applied to the entire population of the United States, the end result would be a very small segment that included Jay. A good niche is one that's specific enough to be meaningful, but large enough to be profitable.

Niches can be applied to both people and businesses. Some widely used filters for people might be:

- Geography: Country, region, state, city, neighborhood.

- Demographics: Sex, age, race, religion, marital and family status.

- Professional: Education, income, profession, affiliation.

- Affinity: Sports played, teams supported, hobbies, community service groups.

Some filters applied to businesses might be:

- Geography: Country, region, state, city, neighborhood.

- Business demographics: Industry, number of employees, number of clients.

- Financial: Size, revenues, assets, profits.

The purpose of these filters is to create a very specific niche. Once complete, you can tailor your business to that niche and market to their needs. Your business may not have as much to spend as the big corporations, but when it comes to your niche, you can outsell and outservice them.

Keep in mind that the bigger your niche, the more competition you have. And the larger the competitor, the more resources they'll have to compete against you. Remember that sales and marketing are a battle of inertia. The more time, energy, and resources you can focus on your niche, the more successful you will be.

How to Make Vital Secret #10 Work for You

You must do four things to identify and market to your niche. You need to identify your ideal client, determine what clients want most from your company, identify how to reach that ideal client, and ensure your sales story and salespeople are consistent with the client, message, and company.

1. Identify your ideal client.
Start by creating a profile of your ideal client. This should be done whether or not you are already in business. As you develop this ideal, consider the following:

- Do you sell your services or goods to businesses, individuals, or both?

- What type of client gets the most benefit or impact from your product or service?

- How much money will the ideal client realistically spend on your business every year?

Describe your ideal client in as much detail as possible. Be specific; outline and segment your points in order of importance. Use the filter lists mentioned earlier in this chapter to help the process.

If you are already in business, rank your existing clients from A to D based on their contributions to your profitability. "A" clients should be the top 10-15 percent, "B" the next 25 percent, "C" the next 40-50 percent, and "D" the bottom 10-15 percent. Take a look at your A- and B-list clients. You'll probably find some common elements in their profiles.

2. **Determine what clients want most from your company.** Develop a message that clearly explains to prospects the benefits your company will provide. Look at your marketing message from your client's perspective by asking "What's in it for me?" (also known as WIIFM). Most failed marketing campaigns create a message that speaks about the company, yet doesn't tell the client why they should do business with the company. For example, which of the following messages is most effective?

- At Big Bob Boots, we pride ourselves on having our boots assembled by our experienced artisans in our plant in Iowa.

- It's time for you to wear the most comfortable, longest-lasting boot in the country. You work hard; you deserve it. Wear Big Bob Boots.

These messages are roughly the same length, and we see variations of both every day. Yet the second message will have a far greater impact on most people. This is because it details how the boots benefit the client, rather than the boots' features. Remember: "What's in it for me?"

The first message creates quality brand awareness, but the second message explains how the boots will benefit the user. They're comfortable, long lasting, and are worn by people who work hard. If you want marketing to create sales, it must focus on benefits to the specific customer. The best way to do this is to develop a short message that tells your story, and then repeat it again and again.

3. Identify how to reach that ideal client.

Just as important as finding the right message is determining the most effective media to use: Are your ideal clients responsive to direct mail? Phone book listings? Newspaper ads? Industry journal ads? Radio or TV spots? Where will each dollar spent have the most effect?

Consider testing each method and tracking clients' responses. Then reach out again and again. It usually takes at least six impressions before a marketing campaign penetrates the prospect's indifference. A great message can actually shorten that time, but even if it does, your marketing will still take several impressions to make a difference. Don't bother spending your money if you don't plan on making advertising part of an ongoing campaign.

4. Ensure the sales story and salespeople are consistent with the client, message, and company.

If you have salespeople, ensure that they are well suited and matched to your ideal client. For example, if your ideal clients are doctors in Denver (such as Jay), you might want your salespeople to have personalities and backgrounds that match those of highly educated professionals in the mountain states. Also, make sure the story your salespeople convey is consistent with your marketing message. The best way to do this is to listen to presentations they make and ensure they reflect your company's philosophy.

■■■■

Vital Secret #11

Referrals are the cheapest and most effective way to get clients.

"Direct referrals from a client are much more powerful than third party professional referrals." Glen is one of the most successful orthodontists in Los Angeles, a city filled with great teeth. His father created a removable teeth aligner (a brace), which has made their practice very popular with adults, including many well-known celebrities. Glen has hundreds of active clients, and sees about 70 a day. Yet because of the nature of his business, the better he does his job, the sooner he loses that client. This success rate forces Glen to find at least 25 new clients a month, all of which are referrals. One day, he and I were discussing how he consistently generates referrals.

First he spoke about third party professional referrals, "I have ongoing lunches scheduled with dentists in my area, mostly around Beverly Hills," explained Glen. "Either I, or one of my staff, will call to tell the dentist that I would like to take them to lunch, and I focus on only those dentists that have good reputations. At lunch we'll talk about our lives, and I'll explain what my practice does and how we work. Typically, I'll let the dentist know that I have many clients who are looking for a dentist, and that I'd like to send him some of my patients if he'd be willing to make some referrals to me."

"For some dentists," explained Glen, "It's all about money. These are the people who say that once they get clients from me, they'll send me some. For others, it's a lot easier and they're glad to enter into a mutual relationship. I try to tell these dentists that what we do is different from other orthodontists and describe the type of client we specialize in, so the dentist will think of us in a specific case. Sometimes I mention an example, like an adult patient who wants to straighten their teeth but is embarrassed at the thought of wearing braces. Once I get a couple of clients, the dentist sees the results over the next six months and typically sends me more."

Since Glen insists that direct referrals are better than third party referrals, I asked him to explain. "Well," he said, "the results speak for themselves, but we have two major sources of direct referrals. The first is when we take a child patient. When I have children for patients, we let the parents come back and sit with us to watch each appointment. In many cases, they'll sit and chat about their own teeth or their spouse's teeth. Over the course of a few visits, they get comfortable enough to ask how we can help them, or someone they know, and they'll often end up becoming clients."

"The second source is when an adult gets their teeth straightened and all their friends ask why they look different, especially since they didn't have visible braces. Our clients' acquaintances are frequently amazed at the results and when they find out that we did the work, they become clients as well."

Glen explained that he always makes a point of letting his clients know if one of their acquaintances has come to visit. "If you do good work," he explains, "it just takes just a little focus to get a stream of referrals."

What Vital Secret #11 Should Mean to You

Every business is constantly looking for more clients. And although the process of getting new customers can be expensive, nothing is as effective as getting referrals from your existing client base or other businesses that share clients with you. Almost every successful service company I've met has some form of referral process, and most successful companies develop an ongoing referral program as part of their business. Those entrepreneurs that didn't have a referral program universally said they wished they did, but that they hadn't focused on it.

The ability to generate referrals is important because referrals are incredibly effective compared to any other form of prospect contact. An industry research firm, Dalbar and Associates, compared and analyzed the closing rate of cold calls and referrals. They found that one in ten cold calls where the person was actually reached resulted in a new client, whereas seven in ten referrals turned into clients. This means that referrals are 700 percent more effective than cold calling. You can imagine that this ratio is considerably higher when referrals are compared to an ad in the paper or a mailer. Yet the cost of a referral is very small.

To better understand the two types of referrals—personal and professional—let's compare them.

Personal Referrals

Typically, a personal referral is when an existing client recommends your company to an acquaintance. This could be when a client tells someone at your company about other people they know who might benefit from your services or products, or even more powerful, when someone tells their acquaintances to come visit you.

In the next section, we'll discuss how to implement and create personal referrals, but there are two universal ways to obtain them. One is to let the client know that you want them, and the other is to simply wow the client. Unfortunately, many companies who are looking for clients do not implement referral programs. The most common reason people do not ask for referrals is because they are uncomfortable asking for them. We'll also show you some key ways to ask for a referral so that everybody is happy.

Professional Referrals

Typically, a professional referral is when someone at another company refers their clients to you. For example, an accounting practice whose clients include small businesses might refer clients to a law firm that works with small businesses. If the law firm agrees to refer small business clients to the accounting practice, the two have a mutual referral program. Another example of a referral program might be an automotive body shop that refers clients to an auto mechanic, and vice versa.

These types of referral relationships sometimes include a referral fee to the business making the referral. We'll discuss ways to foster relationships with other companies in the next section, but it's important to remember this: A referral from another company means that it is putting its reputation on the line, so you must make sure that the company is not put in a compromising position.

Referrals are also a great measure of how well your company is doing. Nothing says your business is successfully meeting client expectations more than continued growth in new client referrals.

Before we discuss how to apply this rule, let me pose the same question that was asked of me when I first wanted to implement a referral program. Have you ever sent a friend to a company you worked with? Why did you do it?

For most of us, the answer is simple. We recommend those who live up to or exceed our expectations. No one feels bad recommending a business or person who did a great job for them or provided exceptional value for the money. Whether it's a painter who did a great job on your house, or a dentist you really respect, we all tend to refer others to people that consistently meet our expectations. Remember that there are two keys to getting referrals: the first is letting the client know you want referrals, and the second is getting referrals from those who are extremely happy with you.

∎∎∎∎

How to Make Vital Secret #11 Work for You

Because the two types of referrals are uniquely different, there are also two different ways to get them. It's necessary to discuss each method separately. We'll begin with personal referrals, and then look at professional referrals.

Personal Referrals

1. Rank your existing clients.

Begin by using the same format we discussed in the previous vital secret: Rank your clients from A to D based on their contributions to your profitability. Again, "A" clients are the top 10-15 percent, "B" is the next 25 percent, "C" is the next 40-50 percent, and "D" the last 10-15 percent. Look at your A and B clients, and identify their common elements.

Ideally, you should target your A- and B-list clients for referrals. This works well because many of these clients are probably friends and business associates with colleagues in similar positions. And as such, their associates would probably be good clients for you. So once you've ranked your clients, consider focusing on these people as potential referral generators.

You should also look for individuals in your A- and B-list that you consider helpers. These are people who enjoy and get psychic income from helping other people. A simple test to determine if a person is a helper is to ask yourself the following: If you were walking along with this individual, and you dropped a pen, would that person reach down and pick it up?

It's a simple test, but quite effective in identifying those clients that like to help. By their very nature, helpers make wonderful referral sources. When they refer they feel like they are helping you and the person they are referring.

2. **Let your clients know that you want referrals.**
There is no single way to do this, but here are some effective statements that have been shared with me.

- "We grow our business by word of mouth; we value the referrals given to us by our valued clients."

- "If you've enjoyed working with us, tell your friends!"

- "Our measure of success is how many people tell their friends about us. Thank you to our valued clients for helping us to grow."

- "Thank you for thinking of us when you or your friends need caterers (or insert product here)."

One of these simple statements placed on a notice in your reception area, on the back of your business card, or on your receipts or newsletter, can make your clients aware that you want and appreciate referrals. This alone often has a significant impact when it comes to generating new referrals.

One of the nicest ways to approach referrals is illustrated in the following example. A particular gentleman sends an annual thank-you note to his top clients at Thanksgiving. The note gives the entrepreneur a chance to show his appreciation to his best clients and closes with a personal paragraph much like the following:

"As you know we grow our business primarily by word of mouth, so I want to give special thanks to our dear clients who thought of us and sent their friends and associates to us to help them with their printing needs. We could not grow without your help. Have a wonderful Thanksgiving."

Every single note is hand signed, and it's hard to imagine anyone taking offense to this note. In fact, it brings this business owner more clients whenever he sends it.

3. **Interact with the referral.**

There are many ways to contact a referral, but your process will depend on what a client is worth to your business and what industry you are in.

- The best kind of referral is when your client has the referral party contact you directly. In this case, it's very important to identify how they heard of you so that you establish this link. It's also crucial that you find out who the referral source is, so that you can compliment that client and communicate how much you enjoy working with them.

- The next best kind of referral is when a client contacts you about someone they believe would be a good client. When this happens, it might be a good idea for all of you to participate in some other activity together, such as having lunch or playing golf. This only makes sense if the prospect could generate enough revenue to cover the expense and time involved. In other words, this might be logical if you're a lawyer, but not if you own a coffee shop. Regardless, a meeting organized by an existing client is a very powerful introduction.

- Finally, there is the case when a client calls you about someone, but doesn't want to introduce you to the person. When this happens, you might want to ask for details about the referral, as well as ask your client to prepare the referral for your call, ideally by calling ahead for you.

4. **Thank your clients.**

If you want to continue receiving referrals from clients, be sure to give them a lot of positive reinforcement. When someone helps you, they want to know that you appreciate their help. More importantly, if you make that person feel good, they'll often continue to send referrals to you. The most common way to say thank you is to send a card with heartfelt thanks. Here are some more imaginative ways to thank your clients for referrals:

- Make a personal phone call. Start or end each day by calling those people that sent a referral and thanking them personally. It can be a very positive beginning or end to your day.

- One entrepreneur makes a point of putting his clients' hobbies in his database. When they send him a referral, he says thanks by sending the client a book on their hobby. His rationale is quite simple; each client is worth several hundred dollars and would normally cost him a lot to find, and sending the client a book on a topic they enjoy helps increase loyalty and encourages the client to send more acquaintances.

- A financial advisor in Georgia sends a wine glass from a well-known New York jeweler. With it, he includes a note that says something similar to the following; "Thank you for sending Dr. Smith to us. We will be helping him with his retirement planning. Please find enclosed a token of our appreciation; it is the first in a set of six." This entices the client to send more acquaintances. The wine glass costs about the same as a book, and creates quite a buzz when it arrives. If the client is a single man, he may send a beer glass instead.

Professional Referrals
1. Identify potential professional partners.
Begin by finding established businesses whose clients would benefit from your services or goods. For example, if you have an auto-body shop, you might want to identify local mechanics who work on cars similar to those you

repair. If you own an accounting firm, identify law practices whose client bases are similar to yours. If you run a coffee shop, look for local companies that would like to enter a relationship with you.

2. Go first—send to receive.

The best way to get a company's attention when it comes to referrals is to send them new clients. For example, let's say the senior partner of an accounting firm meets with the senior partner of a local law firm and asks if they practice estate planning law. Soon afterward, the accounting firm begins sending clients to the law firm, and then the law firm begins returning the favor. When the senior partners meet again, they enter into an agreed-referral relationship. Likewise, the owner of an auto-body shop might enter into a referral-relationship with a mechanic.

3. Come to an agreement.

In these situations, businesses come to different types of agreements. Sometimes, they agree to mutually refer customers to the other business. Other times, a company will offer modest discounts to clients who have been referred from the other business.

Another common agreement is a shared-fee relationship. This means that the businesses agree to pay each other a marketing payment when clients are referred to them by the other business. However, each industry has different codes of conduct, so when considering this option, be aware of legal or regulatory issues. In order to have successful referral relationships, you must know what kinds of agreements as well as legal requirements are common in your industry.

4. Keep the clients happy.

Every business wants to keep their clients happy, but this applies doubly to referral clients. When a business fails to satisfy a client that has been referred to them, damage is done not only to that business's reputation, but also to the reputation

of the business that made the referral. Nothing stops professional referrals faster than treating clients from referrals poorly,
or worse yet, treating them so badly that they call the referring business to complain. Most often, it takes only one such
mistake for your referral partner to stop sending you clients.

5. Maintain a positive relationship.
Also, keep track of how much business is being referred to you
and make sure you let the other business know how appreciative you are of the referrals. Once you know the amount of business you're getting from that source, you'll be able to determine
how much time and energy should be spent maintaining the
relationship, and what level of appreciation is warranted.

Vital Secret #12

Create a self-sustaining sales system.

---

*"One of the great benefits to how we marketed to niches," explained Greg,
"was that we always had leads. Because of affiliations with organizations and
groups, we never had to cold call. And I consider that a pretty big triumph
for us, considering that our salespeople never met clients face to face."*

*In fact, Greg was so successful marketing to niches that his sales team
ran itself. "We had procedures in place to encourage our sales reps to close
transactions, but we also monitored them and followed ethical guidelines, just
as any financial services company is required to do." Greg's company also
built its own customer relationship management (CRM) system to tie their
multiple 800 numbers into their computer database in order to best serve
clients and learn about their prospects.*

*"From a sales standpoint, we were able to immediately see how many
times we'd called that person, or sent them a letter, or when they had last contacted us. Our system also allowed us to touch on all the hot buttons for most
people: what was important to them, did they already have an annuity, did*

they have other investments, what was their net worth, and when they were looking to have an annuity by. All these typical sales questions were worked into the system, so we'd be able to rank the caller based on their sales level."

"That's great," I said. "But how much time do you have to be there?"

"The whole thing ran without me, Joe. I had a sales system in place for both people and customer management. I knew where we were at with all of our customers, and in essence, if a salesperson left, someone else could pick up their workload right where they had left off. Also, most businesses make 80 percent of their sales after the fifth contact with a prospect. But the problem is, your sales team might spend 80 percent of their time making it to the third contact, only to give up. Our system allowed us to manage the process through the fifth contact and make more sales. This was going on day in and day out. Sales occurred with or without me every day."

What Vital Secret #12 Should Mean to You

Creating a self-sustaining sales system means building a sales and marketing machine that generates sales every day and does not require your involvement. In order for this system to be successful, it requires a methodology that brings in new clients, accounts, and revenue in a systematic way.

Typically, a self-sustaining sales system is accomplished in one of two ways. Either a company creates a marketing plan that pulls in new clients, or it builds a sales force to find new clients for the business. Just a few years ago, many companies thought sales teams were no longer necessary because the growing popularity of the Internet would allow businesses to access clients directly through Web-based marketing. As many spectacular flameouts of the dotcom era have shown, this logic does not work for the majority of industries. Today, as in the past, distribution is king. In order to be a valuable player in today's business world, companies need a direct feed to their existing customers, an ongoing ability to attract new customers, and new and evolving products and services.

If you intend to make your business valuable for future acquisition, distribution needs to be one of the most important components. Even if a potential buyer were to have a sales force that overlapped yours, you'd still receive a premium for your business because they would include a future cost reduction in the price of your business. The bottom line is that having a great distribution system is crucial for an ongoing business and is always valuable for a business that is being sold.

So how do you create a self-sustaining sales system, or a constant flow of new customers for your business? There are two distinct ways to do this: pull marketing and push marketing. Pull marketing gets prospects to ask for your product, whereas push marketing pushes your product on prospective clients. Successful companies often use a combination of the two. Let's discuss each in more detail, beginning with pull marketing.

Pull Marketing

Pull marketing is getting clients to ask for your product. With this method, you create a desire for your product by marketing it, through advertising or direct mail for example, and then the prospect comes to purchase your product. As the name suggests, you are pulling clients to your product or service. The same process applies to services. Figure 7.1 illustrates this, using light bulbs as a product.

The primary advantage of pull marketing is the ability to vary expenses. Your marketing campaign can be as costly or as cheap as your business can afford, and you can stop spending money on marketing at any time. Marketing is also relatively easy to implement on a local geographic level.

The biggest disadvantage of pull marketing is the difficulty of implementing an effective campaign. Often, business owners implement a haphazard marketing campaign without tracking its effectiveness or impact.

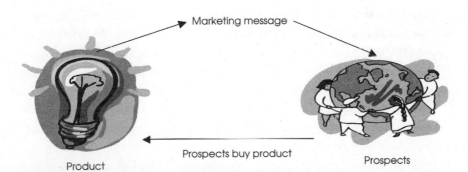

FIGURE 7.1. An illustration of pull marketing.

It's important to maintain an effective pull strategy all the time, or the inflow of customers will slow down.

For example, let's say you just opened a pizza parlor: It's impractical to have salesmen selling your pizza door-to-door because it would waste time, money, and employees. But if you wanted to implement a pull marketing plan, you might decide to mail coupons or fridge magnets to people and businesses in your area. In fact, even if someone orders pizza from you, you should continue marketing to them. Research has shown that mailing to existing customers can be more effective than mailing to new prospects. You've probably noticed that when you order take-out, you often get a menu or coupons from that restaurant in the mail on a regular basis. This tactic serves to remind and entice you to order their food. Regardless of your business, you should allocate a permanent part of your budget to generating new sales by staying in contact with existing customers.

Push Marketing

Push marketing is proactive selling to potential clients. In other words, the client buys the product directly, typically from a salesperson. With this method, a company salesperson meets with prospects either in person or by telephone, and actively seeks to sell them the product by telling them about it. Getting prospects to decide to buy the product is the main focus of push marketing. This process also applies to services. Figure 7.2 illustrates this, again using light bulbs as the product.

The primary advantage of push marketing is one of control. Since a business that uses push marketing typically has a staff of salespeople selling the product, there is a high degree of management control over the volume of sales. The more talented salespeople a business has, the more it can accomplish in sales.

The biggest disadvantage of push marketing is the high cost of developing a sales force. It takes people, as well as all of the tools and collateral materials they might need, to make a sale. Personnel is often the biggest expense of any company. Typically, the better the salesperson, the bigger the expense. And unlike pull marketing, it's much harder to reduce

| Product | Product Sold | Prospects |

FIGURE 7.2. An illustration of push marketing.

these kinds of expenses. After all it's pretty easy to choose to spend less on a marketing campaign, and a lot harder to pare back a sales force. Also, it usually takes a period of time for salespeople to get traction and become effective. Every industry has a different time span for effectiveness, but it's not unusual for six or nine months to pass before a salesperson starts to have a significant impact on your business.

An easy example of push marketing is the insurance industry. A new agency that sells car insurance will need to spend most of its time getting new clients. Since it's often hard to get people to change insurance companies, it may decide to have salespeople, or agents, generate new customers through phone calls and personal interaction.

Comparing Push and Pull Marketing

The key difference between push and pull marketing is the freedom to make decisions. With pull marketing, the decision whether or not to buy the product is left up to the prospect. With push marketing, the prospect is pushed into a decision of whether or not to buy the product. Typically, the more important or complicated this decision is for the potential customer, the more likely that the company needs to engage in push marketing. For example, where you decide to have your shirts cleaned is easy, so pull marketing can be effective in this industry. However it's difficult to decide where to invest your money, so push marketing is more likely to be effective in the financial services industry.

The smartest companies engage in a combination of both methods. For example, major drug companies in the United States practice this. They create pull campaigns for their drugs through advertising, but they spend the majority of their marketing budget developing high-powered sales teams. These salespeople then push the drugs to doctors, who in turn recommend those drugs to appropriate patients through prescriptions. This combination has generated high revenue growth at major drug companies for many years.

Many small businesses begin with limited pull marketing, while the owner becomes the primary push marketer (or salesperson) of the company. As the company grows, the owner can stop pushing the product and begin to develop a specialized sales force.

How to Make Vital Secret #12 Work for You

As with the previous vital secret, the way to create a self-sustaining sales system will depend on whether you're developing a pull or push marketing system. Because of this, let's discuss both in detail, beginning with pull marketing.

Pull Marketing

1. **Develop a compelling message.**

    First, ensure that you have clearly identified your market niche and develop a message that appeals to that specific segment, as covered under Vital Secret #10.

    Also, make sure that your promotion includes a call to action. This means that you always tell the prospect what you want them to do. Returning to the pizza parlor example, perhaps you've chosen to market to everyone who orders pizza within a 5-mile radius for the Super Bowl. You might consider mailing a "Super Pizza for the Super Bowl" coupon to everyone who fits your niche, with clear instructions explaining when the coupon is valid, and when and where to call to order. Remember, every step of any marketing program should try to create a responsive action in response from the prospective customer.

2. Measure and track results.

Over time you'll learn what works and what doesn't, but only if you track the results of every marketing campaign. The keys to gauging the success of your campaigns are time and measurement. Similar to having a handicap in golf, as your marketing gets better, your results should improve. There will be occasional lapses, however, so keeping score will let you measure how well you are doing on a regular basis. If possible, link clients to specific campaigns and measure the effectiveness. Some approaches may not work well initially but could be effective over a longer period of time. For example, the Super Bowl coupon might be very effective for that weekend, but a refrigerator magnet with your phone number might be more effective over a longer time frame.

3. Get feedback and improve.

As you test and measure your campaigns, keep improving and fine tuning them. Marketing is a voyage, not a destination, and your prospects' needs are always changing. Just as different colors come in and out of fashion, different messages will have different appeals at various times. Society is in a constant state of change, and your pull marketing should evolve continuously to reflect this.

Push Marketing
1. Develop a story.

First, identify the benefits your product or service provides to your clients, and weave those benefits into a compelling message. Then boil down your message to its core to come up with your *elevator speech*.

An elevator speech is short presentation that explains your business: It gets its name from the short amount of time people spend on an elevator. If you were on an elevator with a prospect, and you had two minutes to tell them why they should buy your product or service, what would you say? Work on your elevator speech, and try it out on friends and family. Ask them if they feel compelled to buy your product, or better yet, ask them what they would do if they heard this speech. Your goal is to compel them to act.

Let's put together an illustration of this by going back to the insurance example. Assume you're selling insurance to a prospect, and its major benefits are that it's reasonably priced and provided by a highly rated insurance company. What could you say in a short speech that would get the other person to act?

"In these uncertain times, we help people give security to their family. We do that by insuring all the things that you care about, whether it's your home or your health. Since we are all less certain about what might happen tomorrow, isn't it nice to know when you go to sleep at night that your family is taken care of?"

The message here is not about the product, but in a short 30-second speech we've relayed the benefits of our insurance company to the prospect. That message can then be extended to create a 30-minute presentation.

2. Build a sales team.

Next, start hiring people that can sell your product. Throughout my interviews with entrepreneurs, many skills were mentioned as important when hiring a sales person. That list, combined with a review of the hundreds of salespeople that I have worked with, has been distilled down to three personality traits essential to succeed in sales. I've listed these items in order of importance:

- **Persistence.** Anyone can succeed in sales if they are persistent enough. While the next two personality traits are immensely powerful, nothing matters as much as persistence. It is the single thread among every top salesperson

I have ever met. Like that pink bunny with the drum, they keep going, and going, and going. Top salespeople often say that sales is a numbers game and believe that if they ask enough people often enough, they'll bring in business. They're right. If a candidate doesn't believe this, it'll be tough for that person to succeed in sales.

When interviewing salespeople, one busy entrepreneur received a set of resumes in response to a job listing. He completed several interviews, but then didn't follow up with most of them. Afterwards, he received a few follow up phone calls, but one candidate in particular wouldn't let up. Finally, the entrepreneur hired the candidate that pestered him the most, and that individual became the business's top salesperson.

Of course, it's not right to treat people this way, but if you're hiring a salesperson, you must find a way to identify candidates that are persistent. A simple test is to ask them to rank on a scale of one to ten the importance of persistence to success in sales. If they say anything less than eight, there's a good chance they won't stick around long enough to get clients.

- **Passion.** At the end of the day, a salesperson's job is to create action. If they cannot create action, then they simply will not survive in sales. Nothing moves people like passion. It's the ability to transfer and ignite energy that will get people to act. Finding a salesperson that is able to radiate that energy and bring it out in others is very important. A salesperson needs to be able to connect to others, and those that can universally make others feel what they are feeling will be successful.

  A good test to identify a candidate's ability to transfer passion to others is to ask them to tell you about the proudest moment of their lives. A gifted salesperson will take you on a voyage as they share their story. You'll be swept away in the moment and feel all their emotions. As you listen, concentrate more on how you feel than the story itself. If this is a good salesperson, you should feel a rush of emotions. That ability to connect and transfer emotions can happen with your products, but only if your salespeople are able to transmit their passion to total strangers.

- **Confidence.** A salesperson must believe in the product being sold. The more a salesperson is able to convince others of your product, the more others will believe that your salesperson knows what they are talking about.

  Your salesperson must also be able to accept rejection as part of the job and not let it affect their confidence. There are many insecure salespeople in the world, but perception is reality. Some of the best salespeople I've met have been hugely insecure, but are totally confident in front of prospects. Perceived confidence has a huge impact in convincing people, and a person's self-confidence is immediately obvious when meeting with them for the first time.

  For many salespeople, the challenge is to not cross the line from confidence to arrogance. Too much confidence can be as bad as too little, when you're trying to convince others to do as you suggest.

  In addition to your immediate impression, a good test to identify a candidate's confidence is to disagree with something they say, and then watch how they react. They'll do one of three things. They might immediately change their position and agree with you, which obviously does not bode well for their ability to convince others. Or, they might strongly disagree with you and tell you why you're wrong. Unfortunately, this kind of arrogance will alienate many potential prospects. Finally, they might listen to your point of view and acknowledge it before amending their view to include some of your thoughts. This is the response you're looking for, because the ability to find common ground and to compromise requires confidence. More importantly, this ability helps good salespeople overcome objections and as a result close a lot of sales.

3. Compensate based on sales.

People will do what they are paid to do; if you want salespeople to focus on sales, then you need to base their pay on their sales. Sales is the epitome of capitalism. It's not a team sport, but rather a true contact sport; and the best salespeople want to be paid for what they bring to the table, with no limit to what they can make.

When creating a compensation plan for your salespeople, try to provide as little base compensation as possible, focusing instead on large incentives for success. There's often a ramp up time for salespeople to become productive, so you might consider a draw for the first few months. Also, salespeople that want stability and security of income are usually more service oriented than sales focused, so determine what needs you want your salespeople to fill before putting a compensation package together.

■■■■

In the Beautiful Beads story, both sets of girls did what they were asked. However, Ullu and Martha stumbled across a very important secret when they began to approach people whose hands were empty:

Sales is a numbers game; the more qualified the prospects,
the better the numbers.

By approaching only those people without packages, the girls found a group of prospects that were less willing to say no than others, and this realization helped the girls sell far more beads with the same level of effort and less rejection. Remember to fight inertia with focus.

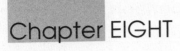

Chapter EIGHT

The Financials

The crucial components that will make your business sink or swim,

and increase its long-term value.

Vital Secret #13

Pay attention to the cash; tomorrow's profits won't pay today's bills.

Vital Secret #14

Focus on generating recurring revenues.

The Money Competition

The Man Who Moved into Town

There was once an old man who moved from the big city to a small town in Namibia. He was well spoken, attentive and gentle. He moved into a little farm on the outskirts of town and drove a five-year-old pick-up truck that had a few small dents but was otherwise clean and reliable.

He spent the first year getting to know the neighbors and many of the people around town. Over time he came to be known as a reliable and generous sort who could provide great insight to those who faced challenges.

On one particular day he decided to post a note on the local bulletin board to announce that he was interested in investing in a local business. He received many responses and he and his assistant placed them into two piles. The first was a pile of letters he called the "I need" group: they came from those who needed the investment to overcome challenges they faced. The second group was the "I wish" pile, for all those people who had reasonably successful companies that needed the money to try to meet a new business opportunity. They were split almost evenly.

He read the first group, the "I need" letters, and was brought to tears by the level of bad luck and despair in some people's lives. He read some of the notes aloud to his assistant who shared in his sadness.

After he was done he sent everybody a note. The "I need" group received a polite rejection letter, while the "I wish" group received an appointment. The letters were all signed by "an investor."

Moral of the story: Charity might go to those who need it, but investments only go to those who earn it.

Students attend school to learn, and their educational progress is reflected in their report cards. While many students dislike being graded, they know that their progress has to be measured. Similarly, in a capitalist society, businesses exist primarily for one ultimate purpose, to make money, and the way to gauge how the business is progressing is through its own report card, the financial statement.

Therefore, one of the skills all entrepreneurs must learn early in their careers is to understand, and to become comfortable working with, the financial aspects of their company.

While many facets of a business are important to a company's success, none is as crucial as financial management. Badly managed financials are almost a certain death sentence for any company.

The challenge for almost all beginning entrepreneurs, except those trained as CPAs, is that this aspect of business requires training and discipline. Fortunately, the rewards of understanding how and where your company makes its money are immense, though not always immediately obvious.

For example, if you spent the morning on the phone looking for new clients, chances are you'd have some success. You'd probably create more sales and generate additional money for your company immediately. Admittedly, there's nothing like instant gratification to make you feel good about how you spend your time.

However, if you spent the morning analyzing your financial statements instead, or did some financial forecasting, you'd see very little tangible benefit to your actions. In spite of the lack of a tangible benefit, you should in no way be deterred from spending time on this side of your business. For example, if you learned which clients made your business the most money, this knowledge could significantly impact future profitability by helping you target your most profitable clients.

When a parent reads a child's report card, they pick up underlying themes about the child's study habits, such as whether he or she is listening in class or making an effort to learn. The same is true when you study and understand your own company's report card. As you review your financial statements, you'll begin to see underlying patterns that need to be addressed and corrected. You might find that your company is spending more on marketing, or that the company's receivables collection has slowed. Entrepreneurs who understand their financials invariably run more efficient enterprises than those who don't. And as time passes, tracking the changes in your financial statements and understanding how each report interconnects is very important. Along the way, you'll find that the only key to becoming proficient with financial statements is practice.

Think back to when you first drove a car. In the beginning it was tough, but with practice driving became second nature. When running your own company, it's important that you commit a block of time to review your financial statements. Over time, this process will be as comfortable as driving a car. Eventually, you'll stop worrying about how to drive the car and focus on getting where you're going.

Financial reports are used in two major ways by independent business owners: for reporting and auditing, and for analysis and forecasting.

1. Reporting and audit function.

This includes the "big three" of standard business statements—the balance sheet, income statement, and cash flow statement. They are all linked; the balance sheet shows the current amount of assets and liabilities the company has, while the income statement shows the most recent period's wealth creation. The cash flow statement reflects how much of the wealth creation turned into cash in the hand. But in many cases, business owners create additional reports that record daily or weekly activity, such as sales reports and expense reports. The main purpose of these reports is to provide a financial snapshot of how the company is doing today, compared to how it has operated in the past. They not only provide a historical perspective for a company, but significant insights into how healthy the company is right now. This aspect of finance is the first area that most entrepreneurs get accustomed to working with. There are many classes and books such as *How to Read a Financial Report* (Tracy Snider) that can give any entrepreneur the basic tools needed to work with these reports. No business owner should simply rely on his or her accountant to take care of this—an accountant can prepare these reports, but the business owner needs to know how to read the report card and decipher what it is telling them.

2. Analysis and forecasting function.

This is the process of breaking financial reports down to the most important aspects of your business, then analyzing their trends and changes over time. For example, you may use your reports to learn what your operating profit margin is, then go one step further and analyze whether that margin is declining or appreciating.

Another example might be to evaluate your marketing expenses as a percentage of sales to give you an idea of whether your marketing dollars are being spent wisely. Some of the questions you might address in the analysis process are: What percentage of your revenue is spent on each aspect of the business? How does that compare to others in your industry? How has it changed with time? What impact does each additional sale make to your profits? How much do you need to sell to break even? This analysis is arguably the most underutilized, but valuable, aspect of financial management for any independent business.

Try to keep it simple; just find the two or three things that matter most. Most successful entrepreneurs realize that a few key "levers" drive their business, and they use analysis and forecasting to find out where they are doing well and what areas need work.

Many important business issues can be addressed and tested through financial statements, and as is the case with most aspects of business, no one has as much at stake as you do, so plan on creating a logical reporting system and spend time analyzing the results. If you begin to constantly ask for answers in this area, your employees will focus on using similar procedures themselves. The two following secrets are crucial to the financial management of your company.

Vital Secret #13

Pay attention to the cash; tomorrow's profits won't pay today's bills.

"As unbelievable as it sounds, all thirteen divisions were profitable. But there we were, burning through cash every day. No money in the bank, almost all of our credit line used up, and I had no idea where our profits were going."

Jeff's firm had 13 divisions, all of them providing services to the entertainment industry, such as equipment rental, talent management, and merchandise manufacturing and distributorship. All of the divisions were profitable, yet the company was running out of cash and headed toward a crisis. As he analyzed each division of the business, Jeff came to the toy and catalog group. Its business consisted of mailing out magazines and catalogs of items they sold to customers. In the past, they had mostly sold toys, but had recently expanded to electronics.

"When I went to the fulfillment center to take a look at what was happening, I noticed a mountain of Panasonic products in our warehouse. We were making a lot of profit on each sale, so we kept ordering larger quantities. I soon found out that we had to pay for all of these expensive products upfront, then carry them in our warehouse until they were sold. This increase in inventory had cost us over a million dollars, and was still growing. So it turned out that all of the cash from thirteen divisions were pouring into a warehouse in Winnipeg!"

Jeff decided to sell the division and learned an important lesson about the difference between profitability and cash flow.

■■■■

What Vital Secret #13 Should Mean to You

The one thing a business cannot survive without is cash. You may have the world's greatest business model, the best sales team, and the most innovative technology, but these things are completely useless if your company does not generate enough cash, or have enough cash in reserve, to continue to pay the bills. Quite simply, cash is the lifeblood of your business.

Our society recently witnessed a great example of just how important cash is. During the Internet mania of the late '90s, plenty of mediocre businesses were able to raise and borrow massive amounts of money in hopes that they would one day change their respective industries and make a lot of money.

As this gold rush passed, it quickly became apparent that most of these companies were spending far more than they could ever hope to make in the immediate future. Of course, once the stock market began falling, it became harder for these companies to raise more cash, which they needed in order to continue operating. Soon, these businesses needed to pay their debt back, and since few were generating positive cash flow, they began to go out of business. One after another, these companies, both big and small, began to crumble. The failure of these dotcoms was due in large part to poor cash management. The few Internet companies that survived kept a reserve of cash on their balance sheet (and in the bank) which allowed them to remain cash-flow positive and continue operating, though often with significantly scaled-back expectations.

When considering extremes, there are two ways to view an entrepreneurial investment in a business and the way cash works in a company.

1. Investing for cash flow.

Some industries and businesses have the immediate goal of generating a cash yield to the owners as soon as they're established. Often referred to as "cash cows," the goal of these businesses is steady cash flow and limited appreciation. Large examples of this are utility companies and real estate entities, while on a smaller scale, companies like dry cleaners, car washes, and restaurants are typically cash flow investments.

Businesses like these can be wonderful to own, because when successful, they provide the owners a stable income stream they can rely on. The challenge to creating a successful cash cow business is keeping enough cash in the business to weather the downturn that will inevitably occur. This means that when taking cash out of the business, the owner must make sure enough money is left in the company to support it during potential slowdowns.

2. Investing for cash appreciation.

Some industries generate a significant amount of capital growth, but don't necessarily generate positive cash flow until a period of time and success has passed. These are cash appreciation businesses, and examples can be seen in the technology and biotech industries. Neither Amazon nor Yahoo made money in their first few years, but both are good examples of this in technology. In the biotech industry, Biogen and Genetech are two successful investment appreciation companies. Smaller examples can also be seen in the manufacturing of new products.

A company whose main goal is capital appreciation needs a large and significant pool of cash in order to sustain the day-to-day operations of the business until it begins to make money. For adventurous individuals, these can be very interesting businesses to own. They offer significant opportunities for gain, but come at a much higher risk to the owner, since they are not being repaid for their work until some point in the distant future.

In the late 1990s, there was an insatiable appetite by investors and entrepreneurs to own businesses with massive appreciation opportunities but limited cash flow. Once the new millennium began, interest returned to stable and less exciting industries. This shift is now bringing attention back to businesses that generate ongoing cash flow streams. Historically, most entrepreneurial businesses tend to be focused on cash flow, since many entrepreneurs do not have access to unlimited amounts of cash. Therefore, they must put their time and resources behind a company that will generate money sooner rather than later.

Once a business is established and operating successfully, the owner must decide whether to take cash out, or continue to invest it in the growth of the business. This is one of the most important decisions an entrepreneur makes, and it often determines the future direction and growth of a company.

Whichever business strategy you choose to follow, never lose sight of the fact that without cash, nothing else matters. To quote one seasoned entrepreneur, "In business, cash is the equivalent of oxygen for a person."

How to Make Vital Secret #13 Work for You

In order to successfully pay attention to cash, you need to do four things. You'll need to take time with your financials, understand the difference between being profitable and being cash flow positive, decide if it is more important to make money today or tomorrow, and share the knowledge.

1. **Take time with your financials.**

   The first step is to learn about the major financial statements and spend time analyzing them. If possible, it's a good idea to ask people in similar industries to share their financials with you. If they aren't comfortable doing that, get some from the public filings of corporations in your industry. Using other reports as a guide, identify the key drivers of your business and develop "key measurement" reports. In other words, try to create a short list of items that give you a quick snapshot of how the week, the month, and the quarter are going.

   Continuing the comparison of a student and his or her report card, some key measurements that gauge if a student is doing well at school would be his or her attendance record, test results, and what time the student went to sleep each night. These things could be viewed as success drivers and measured on a regular basis. Tracking these would give an early indicator of how the student might be faring before getting the report card.

   If you're already in business, you probably know which items are the biggest drivers behind your business. If you're just starting out, find out from peers what you need to look for. Over time, these key measurements can be revised and refined to adjust for factors such as seasonality. But the main benefit of this work is to gain an understanding of how and why your company is where it is, and to help prepare you if things aren't going well.

2. **Understand the difference between being profitable and being cash flow positive.**

   This may seem obvious, but some profitable companies continually struggle because the owner does not understand the timing of cash flows.

This is especially common in manufacturing companies, where small businesses must sometimes offer favorable terms to purchasers. Typically, a small company cannot pass down an increased expense to its employees or suppliers. For example, imagine that a shoe manufacturer has received a large new contract to sell shoes to a department store. However, the department store pays its invoices sixty days after delivery. Obviously, the company would be excited that it had such a large new client, but without enough cash on hand, it could well run out of money during the sixty days of waiting for payment.

This is because the shoe manufacturer must buy the raw materials for the shoes and pay all its employees, wait while the shoes are being manufactured and delivered, and an additional sixty days before getting paid. Despite the wait, the business will still have to continue producing shoes for existing clients. If the company does not have the cash available to pay for the increased production, it could end up in trouble. The company may project a profitable quarter, but end up in a terrible cash crunch. In these situations, it's better to know that a cash squeeze is coming and prepare for it by changing the terms of payment or building a cash reserve, than to be caught off guard and forced to find emergency cash, which can be expensive.

3. Decide whether it is more important to make money today or tomorrow.

The more money you take out of the business today, the less is being invested to grow the company in the future. This also means you'll receive less for it when you sell.

Imagine that excess money (or profits) is being generated by your company. You have the choice of paying yourself a large bonus, investing the money back into the company to hire more people, or advertising to generate more business. How you decide to put the excess cash to work will determine the speed at which your company grows. As you can tell, if you put the money in your pocket instead if investing it on hiring a new sales person or on an advertising campaign, you will not get any growth on that money. Typically, the more money you take out, the less the company will grow.

4. Share the knowledge.

Once you create financial reports, there can be great advantages to including your employees in their review and analysis. The more everyone understands how the dots are connected, the better everyone can identify risks in the future. Someone else might catch a miscalculation that you didn't notice. Simply put, having more eyes review helps to create a system of checks and balances.

Cash is imperative to the success of a business, and in every interview or discussion group we conducted, one universal theme we heard was, "It's better to be pleasantly surprised than under-prepared." In the case of cash management, this statement is exceedingly true. No one will give you the cash you need at a time of crisis without getting a significant premium, so try to be over-funded at all times.

■■■■

Vital Secret #14

Focus on generating recurring revenues.

"I wish it was as easy as I thought it would be," Mark, the owner of one of the largest yoga studios in Southern California is sharing his insights. He has the healthy glow of a yogi. "When we started, I spent so much money on building a great facility that I really never thought about what it would take to bring people in. After we got going, I had to go get the word out that we were opening and all of a sudden, I realized that simply opening a great yoga studio with fantastic teachers wasn't going to pay the bills. I had to get people to come through the door. So we developed a great campaign that got people to come to the studio, mostly flyers that gave students ten days of yoga for ten dollars. People received them and gave them to friends and all of a sudden we had lots of people coming in. The problem was that so many didn't come back regularly. We had to find a way to get people to become returning customers."

I asked why they weren't coming back and he replied, "Probably because they weren't committed and so they found other things to do. We then offered big discounts to people who purchased multiple classes at one time; those students did return and then they would buy new sets of classes with some regularity. Without that base of returning customers providing recurring revenues I had no idea how the business would survive."I asked what he was doing to ensure that this continued and he replied, "It's where all our attention goes. Who are our loyal clients and are they still coming? When they stop coming I call them and tell them we miss them, they usually come back. You have to help people to do the right thing for themselves."

■■■■

What Vital Secret #14 Should Mean to You

Recurring revenue is the ability to get repeat sales from existing customers. In many industries, this is done by charging ongoing fees instead of up front payments. For example, IBM used to sell large computer systems for a fixed price. This was certainly profitable for them, but it also meant that after a customer purchased the system, IBM maintained it, but received no money for doing so. For IBM, this meant new clients needed to be found every month in order to continue to generate revenues. When the economy slowed down, the company suffered a significant slowdown in sales and profits since many clients stopped buying their products.

Their way of overcoming this challenge was to shift to a "fee-based" arrangement (or recurring revenue) with their customers. They did this by charging clients a small installation expense, and then entering into long-term service contracts that extended their service for years. IBM saw the benefits in giving up a large initial payment for a consistent stream of long-term income. The shift allowed the firm to become less cyclical, because even when the economy slowed, they continued to generate revenue from existing clients.

In the airline industry, where fixed overhead is extremely high, the slightest drop in revenue can have a huge impact. Recognizing that repeat flying by loyal customers is often the difference between survival and bankruptcy, airlines developed frequent flyer programs and airline miles to persuade their best clients use them whenever they flew. As a result, these customer reward programs generated significantly predictable revenue streams.

This shift has passed on from industry to industry, and from big companies to smaller players. It has had significant ramifications for entrepreneurs who chose to make the transition, including:

1. **Stabilized projected cash flow and aid in planning.**

   Since all businesses have to make decisions based on their forecasts, the more accurate the forecast, the better the decision. If your revenue stream is reasonably stable, it's much easier to make decisions about any expense, whether it be hiring a new employee or buying new computers.

2. **Increases in service culture mindset and customer satisfaction.**

   When customers are in a "pay as they go" agreement, they must stay satisfied in order to remain clients. This means the company must provide good service and keep clients happy every day.

   The companies that have thrived are those that best service their clients. In fact, even businesses that are not fee-based, but treat customers as if they want a repeat purchase, often generate recurring sales as a result. A great example of this is the computer industry. Dell generates recurring sales because it continues to service clients well after the initial sale. Other computer companies treat each sale as a unique event, so there is little loyalty from their clients.

3. **Recurring revenues that are viewed as more valuable because they reduce risk.**

   In most industries, revenue streams that do not require an ongoing new sale are almost always more valuable than others because they are more predictable and considered to be safer. Whether viewed in the context of an ongoing payment from an existing client or repeat purchases from existing clients, such revenue streams are viewed as more valuable by potential acquirers and lenders.

For example, recurring fee revenues in the financial services industry are worth two to three times more than one-time commission revenue. In other words, a financial company that generates $250,000 in commissions is typically only worth $250,000. However a financial company that generates the same amount in recurring fees could be worth $500,000 to $750,000. This alone suggests that you should push your company towards generating recurring revenue.

The challenge with implementing a shift like this one is the immediate shortfall in income. Obviously, if you opt to defer immediate payments in order to generate an ongoing income stream, you'll need to manage your cash flows well, since there will be an initial decline in revenue. Typically, this process is implemented over time.

■■■■

How to Make Vital Secret #14 Work for You

There are three things you need to do to generate recurring revenues. You'll need to calculate the value of a client, determine if there is a way to generate recurring sales, and ensure that employees understand the worth of the client.

1. Calculate the value of a client.

One of the most important aspects of any business is to know what a typical client is worth. Without knowing this, a company cannot make well-informed pricing or marketing decisions. The best way to do this is to make an assessment of what that client might spend over the course of a year, given that he or she remains satisfied with your business. Then determine the cost of both your service to that client, and the product you sell the client. From this, you can determine the variable operating profit for that client on an annual basis.

For example, let's say Dave owns a butchery. He knows that the typical client comes to his shop every week, and spends $25 each week (or $100 per month) at his store. He also knows the meat he sells to the client costs $50 per month (he has a 100 percent markup), and that his staff typically spends 15 minutes each week (or 60 minutes per month) with that customer. Dave pays his staff $15 per hour, so his variable operating profit per month for a client is $100 minus $50 (the cost of the meat) and $15 (the cost of the employees). This comes to $35 of profit per customer each month. This means that each client is worth $420 annually (or $35 times twelve months). Consider that the person might remain a client for many years, and you begin to understand the value of a repeat customer. In contrast, a client who comes in only one time is worth only whatever Dave made on the transaction.

2. **Determine if there is a way to generate recurring sales.**
   The example illustrates why recurring sales are so important. There are few industries that do not have some way of transitioning to a fee or recurring revenue system. Whether it's giving away the product and charging for the service, such as with cell phones or broadband internet, or creating repeat purchases, such as airlines have done with their frequent flyer programs, there is almost certainly a way for your company to create loyal clients.

3. **Ensure employees understand the value of the client.**
   Every employee in your business should strive to create loyal and valuable customers, because keeping customers happy will ensure profits for your company. Establish recognition programs for your most valuable clients to make them feel special, and get employees involved. There is no downside to everyone at your company knowing what good customers contribute to the business. This will help your employees understand that good clients pay the salaries of the whole company.

Generating recurring revenue is crucial to creating stability in your business. It will increase customer focus and help the company to become more valuable, and what entrepreneur doesn't want that?

■■■■■

The "investor" in the story we began the chapter with was not a cold-hearted person; he was simply focused on making a good investment. All the entrepreneurs I spoke with agreed that it was next to impossible to get cash when they needed it, and that if they did succeed in finding money it came at a very high price. So try to run a cash-rich company that needs only investments, or a loan, to take advantage of opportunities. And always keep a war chest in reserve, just in case.

Chapter NINE

Acquisitions

The secret to making acquisitions that will build your business and

selecting businesses to buy.

Vital Secret #15

Make acquisitions that are an extension of what you do.

The Cost of Knowledge

The Trade

One hot, humid day in the African jungle, a chimpanzee was rolling a huge watermelon past some trees. The chimp was very proud of his find and headed home to eat it, when he heard a voice call to him from a particularly large tree. Looking up, the chimp saw an orangutan hanging from one of the branches above.

"Hey chimp," said the orangutan. "What have you got there?"

"I can't believe it," explained the chimp. "I found this watermelon. I've feel like I've been given a wonderful gift."

"What's a watermelon?" the orangutan asked.

"It's by far the best fruit you can eat on a hot day like this," insisted the chimp. "It's juicy and sweet, and it'll taste wonderful once I open it."

Before the chimpanzee could begin rolling his watermelon again, the orangutan swung down from his branch. "Well, I'd love to try some if it's so great," he said.

The chimpanzee thought for a moment before answering. "I'll tell you what. If you're interested, I'll sell it to you, because my favorite fruit is actually bananas."

"Great!" replied the orangutan. "I've got lots of bananas in my tree, and I'll get some for you if you'll give me the watermelon."

"It's a deal," answered the chimp. "If you'll give me fifteen bananas, you can have this watermelon, and I'll show you how to eat it too."

So the orangutan climbed back into his tree, and brought down fifteen bananas for the chimp. When he came back down, the chimp cracked open the watermelon against a log, snapping it in half. As soon as the orangutan saw the green and pink colors inside, he began to get excited. "Wow!" he said, "It looks really interesting."

"Here," said the chimp, demonstrating how to eat the watermelon. "Take your hand, scoop it in, and then eat the handful." Doing just that, the chimp ate a handful of the melon and spit out the seeds.

Following the chimp's instructions, the orangutan took his hand, scooped it in, and ate the watermelon. But as he ate, the orangutan also swallowed all the seeds.

"No, no," interrupted the chimp. "You shouldn't swallow the seeds. They'll hurt your stomach." Demonstrating again, the chimp took another big scoop of the melon, ate it again, and put all the seeds in the side of his mouth before spitting them out.

Again, the orangutan scooped a handful of the watermelon, ate what was in his hand, but again swallowed the seeds.

"Here," offered the chimp, "try taking a smaller bite. As you eat, put the seeds in the side of your mouth, swallow the watermelon, and then spit the seeds out." After explaining this, the chimp took a final scoop of the watermelon and demonstrated again.

Finally understanding what to do, the orangutan took another scoop, ate it, and spit the seeds out. Happy with his meal, the orangutan began to scoop another handful, but found that the watermelon was now finished. "Ok orangutan," said the chimp as he grabbed his bananas, "see you later."

As the chimp begins to walk off, the frustrated orangutan said, "Hey chimp, do you need any help learning how to eat those bananas?"

"Oh no," the chimp answered. "I've eaten lots of bananas before."

A few days later, the chimpanzee was walking through the jungle, but this time he was carrying two big coconuts in his hands. As he passed the same tree, he heard a familiar voice.

"Hey chimp," called the orangutan from the tree above. "What have you got there?"

"These are coconuts," explained the chimp.

"What are they like?" asked the orangutan.

"They're delicious," answered the chimp. "They have sweet coconut milk inside. The most delicious juice you've ever tried."

Swinging down to the ground, the orangutan said, "I'll tell you what, I'll swap you some bananas for those coconuts."

"Okay," agreed the chimp. "How about 12 bananas?"

Agreeing to the trade, the orangutan brought the chimp twelve bananas for the two coconuts, and as with the watermelon, the chimp said, "Well, I better show you how to eat these."

"No thanks," responded the orangutan. "I remember what happened last time. I'll teach myself."

So as the chimp left with his bananas, the orangutan sat down and began banging the coconuts with his fist. When they wouldn't open, he banged them against a log, against each other, and even against a tree, but nothing worked. Unable to open the coconuts, the orangutan gave up and kept them in his tree until they eventually rotted and were unfit to eat.

The moral of the story: Acquiring knowledge can be very expensive.

■■■■

Purchasing anything requires a certain level of knowledge. Whether you're buying an apple, a plane ticket, or a business, the more you know, the more appropriate a price you'll pay. And of course, the better the price you pay, the better off you'll be.

For common, everyday items such as apples, knowledge is seldom a problem. Just about everyone knows about apples and what they're willing to pay for one. But when buying a plane ticket, there is a huge premium for knowledge. For example, someone who knows absolutely nothing about flying or airlines can pick up the phone, call an airline, and pay full price for a flight. However, if that person spent some time online researching airline prices, reading the travel section of the newspaper for tips and specials, and learning how to get a discount ticket, he or she would acquire enough knowledge to reduce significantly the price for a flight. By gaining an understanding of air travel alternatives, that person might learn that departing from a particular airport or staying overnight could reduce significantly the price of ticket.

When buying a company, knowledge is even more crucial. This is because you'll not only need to understand every aspect of a company you plan to acquire, but you'll also need to apply that knowledge to make the acquisition successful. Acquiring a business isn't like comparing prices for plane tickets. You'll have to understand every facet of your purchase and how it might impact your company beyond the exchange of money.

What you are willing to pay for a company will be a reflection of the current value the business has in your mind. The less you know about the business you are buying, and how it might fit in with your own company, the less accurate your value. When it comes to acquisitions, one thing is certain: The seller wants to get the highest price possible, usually in cash up front. And in that battle of the wills, the one with the least knowledge always loses.

Are Acquisitions Necessary?

Throughout this book, we've discussed several things that are essential to building and growing your business. However, it's important to understand that while acquisitions are not a necessary part of business, they can be important to your growth strategy in your company's development.

It's extremely hard to grow your business exponentially once it is fairly large without acquisitions, and as you grow and gain market share, buying businesses can help turbocharge that expansion. Obviously, you need to make the right kinds of purchases for this to happen, but it is possible to have a strong and growing company with a lot less risk should you choose to never make an acquisition. But if you want your business to grow quickly and rapidly gain market share, making good acquisitions can really help.

The Two Keys to Acquisitions

There are two crucial keys to any successful acquisition strategy. First, knowledge comes at a price, and second, no acquisition occurs without momentum.

As the story at the beginning of this chapter demonstrates, knowledge comes at a price. The morale of the story is that acquiring knowledge can be very expensive, and the orangutan learned what happens when you have little or no knowledge about what you're acquiring. In the case of the watermelon, the orangutan learned how to open and eat the watermelon he'd bought from the chimp, but ended up giving away half of his fruit in the process. When he bought the coconuts, the orangutan chose not to share them with the chimp. This decision meant that he didn't know how to make the most of his newly acquired fruit, and as a result, the coconuts were wasted. In either case the orangutan paid a price for his lack of knowledge of the fruits he was buying.

The second key to remember is that no purchase of a business occurs without building momentum. In order to make transactions happen, you need more than two willing parties—a buyer and a seller. You also need a significant amount of pressure to move a transaction forward. This is because in every acquisition a fundamental conflict exists between the buyer and seller. As the buyer, you want to pay as little as possible for the company you are purchasing, while the seller wants to be paid as much as possible for their business. If there isn't sufficient momentum to keep things moving, the transaction simply won't happen. Both parties must have enough desire to make the sale occur to overcome the many issues that inevitably arise in the process of negotiation.

The bottom line is that when you buy something, you'd better know what you're getting for your money. If you don't fully understand what you are buying and how to use it, you're going to end up paying a huge price.

■■■■

Vital Secret #15

Make acquisitions that are an extension of what you do.

One of the entrepreneurs I interviewed for this book has had significant experience with acquisitions. Mike, a young software programmer who runs a data company, shifted his business to an Internet model in 1999. By 2002, the business had bought eight companies.

"We've had acquisitions that were a perfect fit with our business," explained Mike, "while others have been a bit more difficult."

"For example, one company we bought had a lot of remote technology employees. In fact, this was the business's sole focus. Since we were providing workforce management software to big companies on a nationwide scale, this company extended what we were already doing and made certain aspects of our business easier. The employees of the company we bought were great at what they did, and it was beautiful for both of us. We were able to take over the business's marketing and sales, which were things they didn't want to deal with, anyway. In the end, they were able to focus on technology, which made them happy, and we were able to build upon our existing company, which made us happy."

But not all of Mike's acquisitions turned out so well. *"Another company we bought had what I call a 'Northern California' mentality; the kind of arrogance that came out of technology people in San Francisco in the late '90s. These people thought they were smarter, quicker, and better than tech guys in the rest of the country. As a result, the employees thought they should be paid significantly more than our other employees."*

Mike chuckled as he continued. *"As you can imagine, that didn't fit well with our company. Once we made the acquisition, we ended up taking the company from sixty-five people down to three, and the company's revenues went from five million dollars to two and a half million. But the important thing was that we made the company profitable. It took a lot of house cleaning and ruffled feathers to achieve the goal, but it finally made money, only because we understood the business well."*

■■■■

What Vital Secret #15 Should Mean to You

There are probably three components of your business that a good purchase can take advantage of—your operational infrastructure, your product capacity, or your distribution.

In order to best understand these areas, let's discuss each of them individually, using examples of when buying a company works, and when it doesn't.

1. Infrastructure Acquisition.

The first type of purchase is a size or infrastructure acquisition. In these purchases you want to leverage, or take advantage of, your existing infrastructure. This involves buying a business smaller than yours that can benefit from your guidance. This is also often referred to as a size acquisition.

If you buy a company that is in the same industry as yours, but one-third the size of your company, you already know all of the things that company is going to go through. Because of your larger size, you already have the lawyers, the materials, the suppliers, the vendors, and the accountants, all at probably better rates than the smaller company you might be buying. You also know what it takes to make that business grow.

Imagine you own an investment firm with a billion dollars under management, and you're considering acquiring an investment firm with one hundred million dollars under management. Because you already have the lawyers, accountants, and marketing materials that any firm with one hundred million dollars would need to grow, you can add this investment firm to your business with very little additional infrastructure. In other words, you can simply tuck that business into your own.

At Centurion, we acquired several firms significantly smaller than our own, and each time, we needed to keep only the key relationship people at the company, making the business more profitable than it had been as an independent business.

Likewise, consider this example in the manufacturing industry. Say you own a printing company, and just built a great new printing facility with new presses and equipment. You've spent a great deal of money on the facility, but it's only running at 70 percent capacity. You decide to acquire a smaller printing company to maximize your production. You buy a smaller printing company, close down the older facility, and do all of its printing from your own new facility. In this situation, the purchase takes advantage of the excess infrastructure you want to fill up.

With an infrastructure or size acquisition, you'll typically have a larger infrastructure, deeper knowledge, or cheaper resources than the company you're acquiring (and often you may have all three). When this is true, there are very significant benefits to buying the smaller business.

When It Works

An infrastructure acquisition works when the company you are buying fits very closely with the infrastructure you have in place. In other words, when your knowledge, experience, and operation very closely resemble what the company you're purchasing will need to have in the future.

If you own an investment advisory firm that primarily manages bonds, and you acquire a firm that also manages bonds, you already have negotiated contracts with certain brokerage firms and this allows you to trade them with very small expenses. You also already have researched the majority of bonds around the country, and you already have a sales force that knows how to sell bonds. Therefore, the acquisition could be tucked in with your existing business very easily and neatly.

If you own a printing company, and bought a printing facility that prints the same products as your company and uses the same process you do, only more slowly and expensively, you can move their work into your own facility and make additional profits that the business could not make on its own.

When It Doesn't

An infrastructure acquisition doesn't work when there is a big difference between businesses, or you "stretch" to make a purchase feel logical. A stretch simply means that the acquiring company takes on processes or products that it doesn't understand, and as a result, must make significant changes to its current operating structure in order to make the acquisition work.

Stretches create problems due to a knowledge vacuum. In simplest terms, a knowledge vacuum occurred when the orangutan didn't know anything about coconuts, nor did he learn about them from the chimp. If your business is going into an area where you do not have explicit knowledge about a product or process, especially in an infrastructure acquisition, it's imperative that you gain the necessary knowledge in some manner. You'll either need to hire people that can bring you this knowledge, or you'll need to retain employees from the business you're acquiring. Either path can be successful, but both strategies will also add significant expenses to your business.

Let's imagine that you own an investment firm specializing in bonds, and you buy a company that manages half its assets in bonds, and half in stocks. Managing stocks is going to come with a completely different set of complications that your company has never dealt with. This doesn't mean that the acquisition can't be successful, but it does mean that you're not leveraging your business when it comes to managing stocks. In this situation, you'd have to build a whole new infrastructure for stock transactions. And when you take on areas that your current infrastructure cannot tuck in, you have to spend money to enhance your current infrastructure, which takes away most of the advantages of making the acquisition.

Say you own a printing company and decide to purchase another printing company that's older and doesn't have the scale or size of your business. But let's also say that the printing company has a special binding system that you have no experience with, and because of this, the business specializes in smaller runs of customized work. Although you might be able to fill the excess capacity of your machinery, you're doing much smaller runs. Any of the scale advantage that you had is gone.

2. Product Acquisition.

The second type of acquisition is a product capacity acquisition. In these purchases you want to leverage your existing distribution channels. This involves buying another business to acquire its products, which are then sold through your distribution network.

In the manufacturing industry, you may own a shoe company and have your own internal distribution and sales network. If you buy a smaller shoe manufacturer, you are able to distribute their shoes through your existing distribution and sales network, along with your existing products. The same could be true for a pharmaceutical company that already has a national network of salespeople. If it buys a small pharmaceutical producer, it could sell the additional medical products through its distribution channels, because it already has a sales staff in place that visits doctors and hospitals.

But a product purchase can be about more than distributing a new product through your existing channels. It could also help you maintain your position as an innovator. Whether you make shoes, pharmaceuticals, or anything else, the acquisition could position you as an innovator, because you're introducing new products, even though you've acquired them rather than invented them. American Home Products was one of the world's largest pharmaceutical companies and yet they had one of the lowest R&D budgets. They simply purchased companies with great products and then sold those products through a very strong distribution network.

Most small businesses don't have a huge research and development or new product development budget, and in order to differentiate yourself, you need to consistently offer new products to evolve and grow as a business. So while you may choose to create these products in-house, another option is to buy those companies that make the products that will help your existing clients.

When It Works

Product acquisitions work when you acquire a company that makes products that fit closely with what you are already selling. If you own a shoe manufacturer that specializes in women's shoes, and you acquire a shoe manufacturer that also makes women's shoes, but in slightly different styles, you're likely to be successful. Your distribution channel already knows how to handle ladies shoes, and your sales team is comfortable selling women's shoes. In these situations, the acquisition can usually be tucked in with relative ease.

When It Doesn't

Product acquisitions don't work when you buy a company that makes products too different from what your existing sales force is accustomed to selling. For example, if your women's shoe company bought a men's shoe manufacturer, you are not taking advantage of your distribution network. Since all of your sales are in women's shoes, this can make the acquisition less successful. Your company already holds a certain market segment, and by changing that position through new products, you have to reposition your business, a risky and difficult challenge.

3. Distribution Acquisition.

The third type of acquisition is a distribution one. In these purchases you want to leverage your existing products. This involves buying another business to acquire their distribution channels, which are then used to introduce your products to new customers and markets.

Let's say you own a vineyard, and that your wine is primarily sold to liquor and grocery stores around the country. You're interested in expanding your distribution channels, so you decide to acquire a distribution company that sells wine to hotels. Ideally, you'd sell more wine because it's now being served in hotels for the first time.

Acquisitions of this nature tend to be riskier than the first two types because by extension, you're entering markets that you currently do not work in. Generally, when you make an acquisition that is a distribution play, you're shifting your business solely from manufacturing to manufacturing and distribution. This kind of purchase is designed to give your company new areas to work where you currently don't have a presence. This can work, depending on the price you pay for the acquisition, but it is often disappointing for the purchaser.

When It Works

Distribution acquisitions work when you buy a business that already works very closely with you and understands your product and how it fits into their distribution channel. This often means creating a main distribution channel where the company's client base is already well aligned with your product. For example, if your vineyard makes a very expensive but excellent wine, and the company you're acquiring will distribute it to high-end hotels and resorts, the business could be a good fit.

When It Doesn't

Distribution acquisitions don't work when the acquired company is forced to change its product offerings from several products into one product. Let's say your vineyard only makes red wine, and that you purchased a distribution company that sells many types of wines—red, white, dessert, and cooking. You buy the distributor and then decide that the company will focus solely on your vineyard's wines. This forces the business to cut back from selling dozens of types of wines to only your vineyard's red wines. More than likely, the distributor will lose many of its customers, and your vineyard will not only be unsuccessful in expanding to new distribution channels, but your purchase of the company could fail, as well.

Acquisitions can be incredibly successful, or they can devastate a company. But always remember that acquisitions seldom go as smoothly as everyone anticipates, and that issues you never expected will arise during the process. Most of the CEOs I spoke to said there were never any pleasant surprises when they purchased a company.

Because of this, you'll need to leave a significant amount of room for error. It needs to be a business that you understand well, and one that you can step into and take charge of whenever necessary. In a situation where things don't work out the way you'd hoped, you or a trusted employee will have to run the purchased company. That's tough to do if you have don't have enough knowledge of the business you've acquired.

■■■■

How to Make Vital Secret #15 Work for You

Many companies don't have any acquisition strategy, and those that do usually don't have clear definitions of what they want to buy and why. For these businesses, potential acquisitions sometimes to fall in their laps, and as a result, they're seldom prepared to make an informed and educated decision. If you do not have a specific plan as to what kinds of businesses you actually want to buy, then buying one at random will not help further your goals. Rather, they'll be coincidences that seldom work out as well as buying a company that you've clearly defined and identified as part of your overall business plan.

There are five elements to developing an acquisition strategy: identifying the kind of company you want to buy, developing a financial structure for acquisitions, creating a process to find those targets, building a pipeline to generate potential purchases, and being accommodating and remembering the end goal.

1. Identify the kind of company you want to buy.

The first thing you need to do is identify the kind of company you want to buy. This simply means deciding which of the purchases we just discussed—an infrastructure acquisition, a product acquisition, or a distribution acquisition—would most benefit your business.

This leads us to an important point. Most business owners think of buying a business in one dimension. People often approach this process with the mindset of, "What can that business bring us?" when they also need to be asking the opposite.

The one thing a company you are buying will hopefully bring you is assets. Whether it's a manufacturing plant, money under management, a distribution channel, or a sales team, all these things translate into revenue. Your job after buying the business is to maintain that revenue, and hopefully grow it.

Typically, you should be able to objectively identify what your company does well and find other companies who either do not have these components, whose components are not done as well as yours, or whose components are stronger in different areas than your business.

So what does that mean? It simply means reviewing your company and finding ways to implement your strengths in those companies you acquire. All of the successful examples we've discussed in this chapter demonstrate some of the ways this can be accomplished.

So when you're identifying a company you'd like to buy, you should clearly know

- The size of the business.
- The geography of the business.
- The company's business model.
- The culture of the business that you want to buy.

The more detailed you can be in identifying what you're looking for, the better. Take your time and be as specific as possible, even down to the position of the founders.

It's important to understand that the creation of a detailed strategy will mean you're going to see fewer potential companies to buy, but it also means that the companies you spend time working on are going to be the kind of businesses you'll want to purchase. In the long run, this will save you time, money, and energy.

2. Develop a financial structure for acquisitions.

Next, you'll need to develop the financial structure you intend to have for acquisitions. This means deciding how much cash you can afford to pay up front, what kind of long-term payments you'll want to make, and other financial details.

All of these financial decisions need to be made before you actually begin considering companies for acquisitions, so that you'll have some idea of what purchases your business is capable of making. It is pointless to go out and discuss a purchase with a seller who wants 100 percent of the sale price in cash up front, if you don't have the cash to pay them.

When developing your financial structure, you need to address the four major components of every acquisition:

- The cash component (the lump sum paid up-front in cash for the business).

- The bond, or fixed income, component (the sum to be paid at a later date).

- The equity component (ownership of a percentage of your business you will be giving the seller).

- And the earn out component (paid over time after the sale based on certain targets being met).

The purchase of a business could entail any combination of these four components, and you need to determine exactly how you'd want them set up in an acquisition.

I suggest that when you're building your structure, always include a significant portion as an earn out in some way. Unless the business you're buying is a complete tuck-in, or you don't need to gain any knowledge or experience about the business you're buying, it's important that you include some significant portion of earn out. As a deferred payment over time that is based on certain criteria being met, an earn out will align the sellers with you and provide them an incentive to make sure the purchase is successful.

To better explain this concept, let's look at the previous example of the printing company. Say that you own a printing company, and you've bought a smaller, but more specialized, printing company that provides a type of binding you're not familiar with. If you paid the owner of this specialized printer 100 percent of the sale price in cash upfront, he would probably take his large check, retire, and you'd never hear from him again. You'd be completely on your own in understanding this new process, satisfying customers, and folding in the specialized printer with your existing business.

However, if you paid the seller half of the sale price upfront, and agreed to pay him the other half in increments over the course of the next three years if things work out well, the seller would have an incentive to stick around and help you. You'd have his assistance in converting the existing relationships to your business, and you'd also have his guidance in learning how to operate and profitably run the specialized binding machine.

As you can see, earn outs are a way to transfer knowledge in a productive manner. And as you develop your financial structure, remember that the amount of earn out you pay should reflect how much you know about the business you're buying. The less you know about a business, the more earn out you should be willing to pay. In fact, in some situations where you may know very little about the business you're buying, the earn out may be a majority of the purchase price.

3. Create a process to find companies to buy.

After developing your financial structure, you need to create a process to find companies to buy.

If you consider acquisitions a part of your ongoing strategy, then you should make someone in your business responsible for finding potential companies to buy. Whether it's you or a trusted employee, someone needs to be your business's gatekeeper—the front line of contact for potential sellers and businesses you want to buy.

At first, businesses will seldom come to you and ask to be acquired. Once in a while it happens, but typically you're going to have to be known as a buyer of businesses. This happens over time through word of mouth, especially after a business makes several acquisitions.

The goal is to develop a pipeline that will evolve over time. After you've completed your first acquisition, you'll refine the process.

Without a process to find and develop acquisitions, as well as an individual who is responsible for overseeing them, you'll likely lose sight of and not make any acquisitions in the overwhelming shuffle and rush of your everyday business.

4. Build a pipeline to generate potential acquisitions.

With a process in place to find companies to buy, you'll then be able to build a pipeline of potential acquisitions. Once you've identified the ideal candidate, created the financial structure you intend to implement, and developed a process to get the acquisition, it's time to start building a pipeline. It's also time to be patient.

One of the biggest mistakes many purchasers make at this stage is deciding that since they've done all this work it's now time to make acquisitions. You may feel excited and ready to acquire a business, but don't rush into buying a company just because it is for sale.

Remember the dotcom boom of the late '90s? Almost every Internet company that had gone public was buying companies totally unrelated to their core business simply because they had to grow by leaps and bounds to justify their high stock prices, and as a result, the majority of them made inappropriate acquisitions. You even had traditional companies that vastly overpaid for assets they didn't understand at all, simply so they could have an Internet presence. Many of those companies fell in value by 95 to 100 percent. Sometimes the timing isn't right, and sometimes a particular industry gets ahead of itself or pricing gets out of control. There's no better example of that than the Internet. So be patient.

Buying businesses can also give you insights into your own market. As we negotiated acquisitions with firms typically smaller than ours, we learned new ideas and concepts that could apply to our own business.

Even if we ended up not buying a particular company, we would catch a business concept or learn about a market that we would not have thought of. So acquisitions in and of themselves can give you a huge advantage in learning about your industry and what's happening at other businesses. In fact, every time you negotiate with a potential purchase candidate, you are learning and educating yourself about their business. And in essence, while you should never violate non-compete and non-disclosure agreements, you will still gain from the experience.

5. Be accommodating and remember the end goal.

Finally, be accommodating and remember your end goal. During the process, once you've actually identified the right candidate and started negotiations, it's very important to maintain focus, a sense of humor, and momentum. There are times in most transactions when the acquirer finds his patience tested by the never-ending requests of the seller. When this happens, remember that the seller is offering you their life's work. So if you truly want to acquire the business, being accommodating, having a sense of humor, and remaining focused can help you complete the acquisition. The less flexible you are, the higher price you'll pay.

A Sample Process

Once you've found a business you want to buy, you need to follow a simple process such as the following: Negotiate with the seller, develop a term sheet for the purchase, complete due diligence of the business, and formalize the transaction.

Time is also a factor. You should strive to keep this process as short and manageable as possible without compromising the integrity of your due diligence and research. Doing so will keep everyone focused and ensure that the process is not open-ended. So although you shouldn't rush, there should be a finite window of time for developing and agreeing on terms. The important thing is to not leave the process open ended, so that momentum continues, the acquisition progresses, and things get done.

■■■■

All successful acquisitions are based on knowledge and leverage. They are part of the American way of doing business, and they are exciting. And although buying companies can be an attractive way to grow in size, the process itself is seldom easy. Business owners talk about leverage and how acquisitions take advantage of what you already have, but unless you have the knowledge and experience to utilize the business you are buying, the acquisition can come at a very high price.

Acquiring knowledge can be very expensive.

We began this chapter with the story of the chimpanzee and the orangutan. And as the orangutan learned, you need to learn what you don't know, or you will certainly pay a price for a lack of knowledge. The less you need to be educated, the better the acquisition will be.

Chapter TEN

How I Sold My Business

The story of how my partners and I sold our business, and how selling

your business is a lot like getting married.

Listen Right

The Tale of the Flying Monkey

Deep in the jungle of Africa there lived a monkey who loved coconuts. The juiciest coconuts he could find were at the top of a very tall tree in the middle of a grassy field. But since the coconut tree had no branches, the monkey could not climb it. Every day, the monkey would look up the tree, stare at those coconuts, and wish he could have one. Once in a while he would try to climb the tree, but after climbing a few feet he'd slide down the trunk. At the end of each day, elephants would come to the pasture and the monkey would run off.

After a few days of frustration, the monkey went to get advice from the wisest creature in the jungle, the owl. When the monkey asked the owl how he could get to the coconuts, the owl replied, "Well, I would get there by flying."

"But I don't have wings!" said the monkey. The owl suggested he make some. "But how?" asked the monkey.

"Well," lectured the owl, "I've read that banana leaves stuck together with honey work pretty well."

So the monkey ran off to gather the necessary equipment for his wings. While he was gluing the leaves together, a mouse came by and asked the monkey what he was doing. Once the monkey told the mouse about his conversation with the owl, the mouse chuckled.

"You know those coconuts sure are a long way up," the mouse said. "And if you want the coconuts I can show you how to get them."

"What do you know?" interrupted the monkey. "You're just a mouse. You can't fly. Besides, the wise owl has told me how to get to those coconuts, so leave me alone."

Later that afternoon the monkey climbed to a nearby tree, his new wings intact and ready for flight. He looked across the field at his prize and at the elephants gathering below. He took a deep breath and jumped.

He flapped his arms furiously, but nonetheless the monkey fell to the ground. As he lay nursing his injuries, the mouse walked by and handed him a juicy piece of coconut. "You know," he told the monkey, "if you'd just waited for the elephants, when they rub themselves against the tree they shake the ripe coconuts down."

The moral of the story: Listen to the wise, but trust the experienced.

■■■■

GE's Financial Assurance agrees to purchase Centurion Capital Management, an investment advisor based out of Sherman Oaks, California.

New York Times,
October 17, 2001

Well, it sure looks trivial! Relative to the scope of everything else going on in the world at the time, this was barely a blip on the national news front. Yet here it was, the culmination of ten years of work and millions and millions of dollars all reduced to a couple of lines in the New York Times and the Wall Street Journal.

When all is said and done, and you share your success with friends and family, you're going to get a lot of compliments and pats on the back. "Boy, you are one lucky guy," they'll say. "Wow! It's amazing. It happened so quickly," you might hear. That's because from the outside looking in, it all seems very easy. If you, your friends, and business associates get to read the blurb in the newspaper stating that you sold your business to Big Corporation, Inc., nowhere in that text will it describe the extremely tough and arduous process it took to make that happen—the negotiating, the due diligence, the late nights, and the actual transaction—all of which has to happen while you manage your existing business. There's certainly no mention of the years it took to make your business valuable in the first place.

Newspaper blurbs don't show you all the machinations that go on behind the scenes. For my partners and me, one of the disadvantages we had in the negotiation was the amount of esteem and admiration we had for the company that was acquiring us, General Electric. They were so much bigger and better prepared than we were and had done so many acquisitions, that they handled the process like a well-oiled machine. We, on the other hand, had never been on the sellers' side of the desk before.

Just as we had the advantage in our past, when we were the acquirer of companies, we were at a huge disadvantage when it was time to sell because we'd never done it before. GE acquired a large number of businesses every year, and had a process in place they were accustomed to using. They knew exactly what was going to happen and when, while we were in the dark. This was 10 years of work we were selling, but it was just one of many acquisitions for them.

■■■■

In Chapter 1, I compared the growth of a business to that of child growing up. As I look back at our dance with GE Financial, I realize it followed a particular pattern not unlike the courting ritual of two people. There are clearly defined steps to take when selling your business. Therefore, I'm going to compare the steps involved in selling your business to the same events you'd go through to court someone for a marriage.

1. The introduction, when you meet someone that might be a good match.

2. The dating period, when you learn more about that person.

3. The engagement, when you make a formal commitment to each other.

4. The marriage, when you complete the relationship and actually join together.

Although we're going to use the relationship analogy, there is a major difference: There is seldom a natural increasing progression in the transaction sale of a company. It will require constant pressure to develop the transaction. As the owner, this is what you are striving to accomplish: *to maintain a good impression and to sell your business.*

This process can take weeks, or most often months. But regardless of length, it will almost certainly be a stressful process for the business owner. However, the more you keep focused, the more likely you'll succeed.

1. The introduction, when you meet someone you're interested in.

In 1999, our investment bankers, Putnam Lovell, created a venture fund to invest in financial services companies. Most of the investors for the fund were principals of the investment bank who asked if they could invest in our company. At the time, we had plans to do several acquisitions and knew this additional capital would help, but since Werner, one of the founders, wanted to get out of the business, the majority of the money they invested would be going primarily to him instead.

We got a little more money to invest into the business, but more importantly we also got a well-known investment banker as an investor, which gave us the opportunity for a significant line of credit with a large bank for our planned acquisitions.

Putnam Lovell made a second investment in our company a few months later, but this time they were investing on behalf of several large financial institutions. We viewed this as an opportunity to meet companies we might one day want to sell to.

Because of the quality of the investors, we were willing to take the investment at a price we thought was slightly below the value of the business. The way we saw it, this was a great opportunity. We would give these investors a small percent of the business at a reasonably low price to get them involved, make them money, and hopefully if it all worked out well, one of them would want to buy us. We were very confident that 2000 was going to be a good year. Unfortunately it was the beginning of the terrible bear market that would continue for several years.

The introduction period is basically the breaking of the ice. When you're dating, you don't intend to marry the first person you meet, and likewise, all we wanted to do was find the right group of people to associate ourselves with—people who might end up as future partners.

In many ways, the investment bank was like a matchmaker. If you hired a matchmaker when you're dating, you'd tell them what kind of person you're looking for. You might say you want a non-smoker who likes to work out and is within a certain age range. You might even tell them the hair color you like. In the same way, we had very clear descriptions of the kinds of companies we wanted, and the investment bank not only found companies that met our requirements, but they had ideas that never occurred to us. That's not to imply that all investment banks will provide these insights. I have found over my history that many bankers act like car salesmen, simply focused on making a transaction. In our case since they were investors in our company, they had a financial interest in really helping us.

2. The dating period, when you learn more about the person.
In early 2001, the folks from GE Financial asked if they could come and visit our offices. "You have an interesting shop," they told us, "and we'd like to see how you grew so much last year." At the

time, most financial service firms were facing challenges. The year 2000 had turned out to be tough for the financial industry, and 2001 was looking to be more of the same. However we grew our company by 100 percent in 2000, through acquisitions and good sales, and 2001 was going well for us too. They wanted to learn what we were doing.

From the way they presented it, I was expecting an informal visit—just a couple of people who were going to be in town. Then they told us the weekend before they arrived that 10 people were coming from GE Financial, which meant there was a significant chance they were coming to do more than chat. When a company sends that many people to see the business, they're not casually dropping by for lunch.

The meeting was set for the following Monday, and my partners and I realized that we were not at all prepared for an initial review visit. Not surprisingly, we spent the weekend working on a formal presentation. My partners and I sat down, decided who was going to do what, and put a presentation together. On Sunday night, we got together for dinner and went through everything, making sure we were ready for the following morning. We were like a freshman going on his first date, and it's with the homecoming queen!

Just like a first date, we did everything in our power to make sure our first impression was going to be fantastic. We had everyone come into the office early, and everything was brushed and polished. I also did a lot of work learning about GE Financial and how they positioned themselves. I spent time on their websites and talked to people who had worked for GE to make sure our presentation truly resonated with them. I found that the three things GE stands for are quality and innovation in their products, having the right kind of people in the firm, and last but not least, being profit driven. I made sure the presentation reflected those values.

On Monday morning, we had a really great session that lasted roughly six hours. A few weeks later, we got another call from GE Financial, and they said, "We'd really like to do another meeting, nothing serious." This time, they came back with a different set of people, and we were ready for them. Since we'd already given the presentation once and it'd gone quite well, we basically repeated the same thing.

At this point, we were presenting to the decision makers and the dealmakers from GE Financial, but the interesting thing was that we didn't really know who was who. Like the prior presentation, our meeting went well. After all, who doesn't behave well on their second date?

■■■■

The dating period is basically about making a good impression and making sure the other person is interested. When you go out on a first date, you're sure to look, sound, and act your best. This was the case with every entrepreneur who sold their business. They wanted the potential buyer to be impressed and to want to pursue things further.

3. **The engagement, when you make a formal commitment to join together.**

For the next few months, my partners and I worked on negotiating a term sheet with GE. They wanted us to be exclusive to them while we were in discussions, so we took ourselves off the market. What was amazing to us is that we rather naively thought it wouldn't take long to come up with a term sheet, and that the necessary due diligence might take a few weeks. We actually started by saying, "It'll take a couple of weeks to negotiate the term sheet, then ten days of due diligence where they'll come in and make sure everything is the way we say it is, and we should be done by April or May. No problem."

Well, I had planned a great family vacation with my wife and kids in July. I'd saved up all my frequent flier miles, and we were going to London and France, where we were meeting up with the rest of my family from Africa. We'd rented a house in the south of France and were planning on a great summer. With the sale behind me we would have a really great vacation.

May came along, and we were still in negotiations. June also came and went with only modest progress. Every time we set a deadline for something, we seldom met it. Sometimes we didn't speak to each other for several days. We came to realize that we had no control over the timing or scheduling of the negotiations, and things were completely at GE's control. The power is almost always with the buyer, and since we had taken ourselves off the market we were at their mercy.

To keep ourselves focused, my partners and I had a belief while negotiating: "Nothing is going to distract us from getting this deal finished." You have to keep the momentum moving forward. You can't let a couple of days go by without having a conversation with the buyers. The whole process literally ebbs and flows. One week we felt like we were doing great, and the next week we thought things were slipping though our fingers. I was 33 at the time, and we were talking about huge numbers. It was mind bending, exciting, and incredibly intense. Meanwhile, we still had to operate and run the business in the middle of a bear market. Fortunately during this time, we were doing really well for our clients.

We knew though that if we didn't get the deal done with GE Financial, we weren't getting a deal done with anyone else. Financial companies were doing so poorly at the time that they couldn't afford to make acquisitions. By July of 2001, we knew that it was now or never. The bear market was showing no signs of changing, and the price for asset management firms was coming down. As you can imagine, investment firms are a lot less attractive in a bear market, and we were being offered a price that we probably weren't going to see again for many years, even if the business got a lot bigger.

In August when it was time to conduct due diligence, a huge group of people showed up. A team of lawyers from the East Coast arrived. They spent weeks asking for an endless barrage of information. The laundry list of information we had to provide was beyond anything you could imagine. It was thousands of pages; every contract, every file, everything we'd ever done during the preceding 10 years they wanted to see. And not only did they end up looking at absolutely everything we'd ever done, but they usually had two or three people looking over every document so we'd have to send copies. Fortunately, we'd assigned a very capable team of employees to coordinate their efforts with our staff.

By mid August we had negotiated a very complete term sheet and all that was left was drafting final documents. We managed to satisfy their requests. Everything was finally negotiated by 9:00 p.m. on September 10, and I came home and told my wife the good news. "Honey, I think we're done," I said, and she asked if we should open the bottle of champagne we'd been saving in the fridge since the beginning of negotiations.

"No," I told her, "let's wait until we get the contracts faxed tomorrow." The next morning we were going to receive from GE the definitive agreements that signaled a formal engagement.

Sadly, the next day was September 11, 2001. That morning I was getting ready for work as I watched the financial news channel. While I was shaving I saw the first plane crash into the World Trade Center.

The next three weeks we didn't hear anything, and during that time my partners and I assumed the deal was off. After all, the stock market was completely decimated when it opened two weeks later. The good news was that our clients barely lost money the week the markets reopened. We had very defensive strategies that helped protect them in bad markets, and our inflows of new assets increased significantly after September 11.

"The deal is over," I remember thinking. "We're going to have to run the business. Fortunately our investments are working well, but the whole world is different now, and our company is probably worth half of what it was. So we've got to muscle through. Our attention was distracted for some time, and now we're going to have to concentrate on our core business."

But fortunately GE did call back. A few weeks after the tragedy, we got a call from an employee who asked for a report on how things were going for us. We put together a quick report showing the improvements in performance, sales, and new accounts over the past few weeks and sent it over. Once GE Financial got the report, we got another call from someone higher up who asked, "These numbers look nice. Are they accurate?" Without hesitation, we told them the numbers were indeed correct.

So after another couple of weeks, they said they were ready to renegotiate, but because of the recent review of the company, they wanted to make some adjustments to the price. I didn't like it; our business was in better shape now than at any point during the past 10 years. It didn't feel right at the time, however looking back I realize my ego was in the way.

But we had a conversation with GE Financial, and they told us exactly what they'd be willing to do. Afterwards, we had our own offline call with our investment bankers.

"But do we want to stick around for another five years before we are able to sell again?" Bob, the Chairman and my mentor asked. They asked me what I thought the market was going to do, and I told them my perspective. "It's going to be very tough for some time because the market has probably not yet priced in what September 11 means to the economy."

"How do you feel about the grinding away for the next five years to end up in the same place?" he asked me. "I'd rather have the cash in my pocket than the company," was my answer, and we all felt the same way. So we called our bankers back and said, "Let's go close."

■■■■

The engagement period is basically about making a commitment to each other and being sure that both your needs and expectations fit with the other person's. By the time someone proposes, a couple has already talked about their plans for the future, such as where they want to live, how many children they want to have, and what they want to do. Likewise, the term sheet and negotiation of the definitive agreement allowed both us and GE Financial to clearly state our expectations and needs in order for us to sell the business.

During the engagement period, people often have mixed feelings constantly tugging at them. Is this the right one? Am I ready to settle down and spend my life with this person? We had the same feelings. "Is this it? Are we happy with this offer?" With every week that passed, my partners and I kept getting stuck on one thing or another. Sometimes it was the pricing, while other times it was a term or condition, constantly pushing us to the point where we'd be willing to walk away.

4. The marriage, when you complete the relationship and actually join together.

Although we thought the negotiations and scrutiny would be over once we decided to close, the gives and takes continued week after week until mid October. At this point, the GE Financial executives flew out to finish things up. The plan was to have dinner with them that night, and then meet to sign the legal paperwork at nine the next morning.

Once the GE employees arrived, they met us at our office before dinner. Within minutes, they informed us that they had found one issue that would require one more change. Even though they gave us what they considered to be a legitimate reason, we felt like this was the final straw.

My partners and I sat in a room together to discuss this latest demand, and frankly, we were right at the tipping point of walking away. At that moment, we weren't even sure we wanted to go to dinner with them. I arrived before my partners, and at dinner, I conveyed our frustration. "You've pushed us right to the point where this no longer feels good to any of us," I remember saying to the group. They probably knew then that they were at the best price they could get.

But the next morning, we acquiesced and showed up at the law firm to sign the documents. We expected things to go quickly, and in fact had all planned to meet at nine, sign and be out by ten in the morning. We ended up staying there for 18 solid hours, until three in the morning the next day! That whole time, the GE Financial executives kept pushing their flights back. At first they were supposed to catch a one o'clock in the afternoon flight, then a four o'clock flight, and finally a nine o'clock at night flight. In the end, they flew back the next morning. But my partners and I knew if we left those offices without signing the transaction, it wasn't going to happen.

During this time, we had a conference room, and they had a conference room, and literally we went back and forth for the next 18 hours. Every time we'd make a change, they'd go over the whole contract again, catch things that were inconsistent, and we'd have to change something else. The final contract was quite complex, because whenever one of us would consent to something, it would mean a complete rework of the whole agreement.

At times, we would sit in the conference room waiting for over two hours, and unfortunately, our lead counsel who helped us through the whole process had to leave because of an unexpected family crisis. Before he headed out the door, he told us, "Remember the movie *Glengarry Glenn Ross*. ABC—Always Be Closing. Don't leave without having their signatures on the contract. I mean it, ABC." It was great advice, because whenever one of us started to get really annoyed, we'd remember "ABC." He left at about 2:00 p.m., and after another 13 hours of negotiating, we finally were done. There were several times when we thought we'd hit an impasse, but we kept moving forward through the standoffs.

I finally got home around 3:30 in the morning. I woke my wife and told her the good news. I slept like a log for three hours, but the next day I had to get the word out and begin the process of converting the company over.

Although the transaction was complete, we had to get consent forms signed by all of our clients. This took about two months, and we were going to be officially part of GE Financial on December 17. On the morning of December 15, my partners and I flew to New York, where we met with the folks at GE Financial and went through the paperwork. At the lawyer's offices, the closing paperwork covered a huge conference table. Stacks and stacks of paper were laid out, and we went through everything. However, there were a couple of issues that still weren't quite right.

It felt like I was in an ocean and the rescue helicopter kept dangling a cord just within my grasp but the wind kept blowing it away. After a restless night, the problem turned out to be something relatively trivial, was corrected, and the next day, the wires were authorized again. Both excited and worried, I called my banker every 30 minutes to see if my wire had arrived, and every 30 minutes, he told me it hadn't come in yet.

By the afternoon, my partners had gotten their wires and I was about to leave for a meeting I'd scheduled. My payment had not yet arrived. During my meeting, I was completely unable to relax or focus. My money was being sent right before the wire system closed for the day, which is around mid-afternoon.

After the meeting, I called my banker, who said, "We've got the last batch, but I don't see it." Soon I was at my wit's end, when I finally got a phone call from my broker. "We've got one more wire here, and it's for millions of dollars."

"Hallelujah!" I told him.

After getting off the phone, I went for a walk. Trying to relax, I had a strange feeling in my stomach. I felt as if the whole process had been so gut wrenching, that by the time we got our money, it almost felt anti-climactic. Wanting to buy something special for my wife to celebrate, I walked into Tiffany's. But as I looked at all this great stuff, I realized the money and gifts were meaningless compared to being with her and my precious little daughters. Strange as it might sound, all the money in the world meant nothing compared to being with my family. There's a lesson in there that I've heard from all who have sold a business: When you're in the heat of battle, don't lose sight of what you're doing it all for.

Once dinner with the folks at GE was over, my partners and I had drinks at the Plaza Hotel, saluting our good luck. It wasn't until that point that we looked back and realized how many things could've gone wrong—how many things could've kept the business from succeeding. It was then we realized that we were unbelievably lucky. We'd worked hard to get it done, but we were also extremely lucky. As I flew home from New York to Los Angeles nothing mattered as much as seeing my girls. It's hard for me to imagine how I would have felt had I not had my family to share this success with.

■■■■

The marriage period is the formal commitment and final step in the process. And just as you may have butterflies in your stomach on the day you get married, going through with the sale of your business can be extremely stressful. Also, just as marriage changes who you are, your relationship to your business changes once you sell it.

We will talk more about post-sale at the end of the book but to conclude, I ended up working for GE Financial for a little while. I was made president of the division that oversaw my former business, but the company had its own ways of doing things, which were quite different from the way I'd done them.

I recognized that my business belonged to GE Financial now. I also realized there was no longer a place for me as the former leader of the business. This might well be true for you, too. Your employees may still look to you for guidance, but you're no longer the one to provide it. Personally, it's a difficult spot to be in, and the hardest part of the process.

That's when I really got a sense that it was over—once I realized that strategic decisions were going to be made away from me. And once you've run your own business, it's very hard to go back to being an employee.

So I left my new job with GE Financial, which was difficult to do. On my last day a procession of people came into my office to say goodbye. To this day, I still get calls every week from people who worked with me.

The thing I'm most proud of was our ability to grow a business to that size, and that everyone truly loved working there. They all knew that with my departure, things were going to be different. What made me feel better than anything else about our business was this—we'd created a valuable entity. Because of the people we'd put together and the culture we'd created, we'd built something out of nothing. Alchemy!

■■■■

So what should my experiences mean to you? Well, there are some insights that you should keep in mind.

First, the process definitely takes much longer than you'd expect. You need to have absolute intensity and maintain your momentum to make the transaction occur. Just like we had a business to operate, GE did too. It certainly wasn't as if they had to acquire our business. You'll have to keep your buyer excited about doing an acquisition while also staying focused on your business. And no matter how long things take, you've got to keep the momentum rolling.

Also, be realistic about your price and expectations. If you're successful, you'll eventually get paid a close approximation of fair value. If you're expectations are too far away from fair value, you're going to sit on the market. When our sale was announced, it was a multiple few people could believe. The price we got was well above industry norms, but we'd also created major differences between us and everyone else. I believe our business had been built to be more valuable.

We were also very focused on controlling things we had power over, one of which was asking for as much as possible in cash upfront. This was because once the business is handed over, you won't have any control over the earn-out. I was pretty certain GE Financial wouldn't want my partners and me running the business. And if that was the case, how much control would we have had over how much we were going to get paid? We did not want to negotiate with GE Financial over what we were owed two years down the road. We didn't want to be at the mercy of our buyer when it was time to get paid. After all we were an ant and they were an elephant; it wouldn't exactly be a great debate.

Finally, be prepared to give up control. A company that's in the process of buying your business will never tell you they don't want your help, but after the sale this will probably change quickly.

Most importantly, keep the end result in mind. You've made the decision to sell your business rather than continuing to run it yourself. There will be times of stress, late nights, and exhausting work. But stay focused and keep working, because once it's over you'll have achieved your ultimate goal. As mentioned earlier, though, don't lose sight of what you did it all for and the people that matter to you along the way.

We started with the story of the flying monkey. You will be given lots of advice while you are in the process. Stay focused on the advice of those that have lived it. It is very hard for someone who has not gone through a transaction to really understand what you will go through. Try to keep the sale in perspective. You don't want the negotiation to endanger the rest of your relationships, the ones you want to live with after the sale. This is hard, but crucially important if you want to maintain a good life after the sale. The remainder of this book includes the advice and insights of other business owners who sold their company from a couple of million to many millions of dollars, and the remaining secrets to selling your company for the highest possible value.

Chapter ELEVEN

Preparing Your Business For Sale

The secrets behind getting the highest price for your business

and enticing buyers.

Vital Secret #16

Make yourself dispensable.

Vital Secret #17

Sell when things are going great.

Vital Secret #18

Reward the people that are important to the transaction.

Selling High

Donkeys at Market

In a village in Zimbabwe lived two brothers who had just taken over the family business. Their father, who had recently passed away, handled many of the tasks necessary to support his family, and the brothers were now taking on his responsibilities.

The family owned many donkeys to help with the farming, and sometimes their father sold one at the local market for extra money. The family was now in need of money, so the brothers decided it was time to sell a few donkeys themselves.

The older brother, who had many friends and enjoyed traveling and meeting people, said, "I'm the oldest. I'll do it." So he went and randomly grabbed one of the donkeys, and walked to the market. Once he got there, he began to create a lot of excitement about the donkey. He approached people, showed them the donkey, and loudly told them what a fine animal he was selling. Soon the older brother had a crowd watching him. He seemed to be a natural salesman.

Soon, though, people began looking closely at the donkey and realized that it was in poor shape and old. Because the older brother had spent so much time away from home with his friends, he never learned about donkeys and had picked the worst one to sell. After selling the animal for only $25, the older brother came home.

Upon returning, the older brother was told by his younger brother, who was shy and quieter than his brother, said, "You should've picked a better donkey. That's why you didn't get much money."

"If you think you can do better, go ahead," the older brother replied.

So the younger brother went to pick out a donkey to take to market. Because he had spent much of his time at home, he had learned about many things from his father, including donkeys. To make sure he picked the best donkey the family owned, he carefully looked at each donkey's tail, teeth, coat, and hooves. Having finally made his selection, the younger brother headed to the market.

Once he arrived, the younger brother quickly realized he had the best donkey around. So setting up a stall, he brushed and cleaned the donkey, then sat down and waited for interested customers. But as the day went on, no one came by. The younger brother was frustrated because no one seemed to be interested in this great animal.

Finally, a shopkeeper who'd been watching him came up and looked at the donkey. "I'll give you twenty-five dollars," he said.

"Come now," responded the younger brother. "Surely, he's worth more than that. Just look at his teeth, his coat, his hooves. He's a great donkey! He's worth more than that."

"Perhaps," said the shopkeeper. "But there's no one else here. I've been watching you all day, and no one else has even come up to you. So why should I pay more for this animal when no one else wants to buy it? If it's as good a donkey as you say, there'd be more people here offering you money."

Admitting that the shopkeeper was correct, the younger brother sold the donkey for $25 and walked home.

After hearing of his brother's misfortune, the older brother said, "Well, then, the two of us should try to sell a donkey together." So the next day, the two brothers went out into the pasture and the younger brother again selected the best donkey the family owned. After walking to the market, the older brother began creating interest in the donkey, speaking to people and drawing a crowd.

Soon, the brothers had many customers interested in the donkey, and they sold it for more than $50. That day, the brothers decided they'd work together whenever the family needed to sell a donkey.

The moral of the story: Getting the highest price requires both salesmanship and a great product.

There is a difference between a business that's easy to operate and a business that's easy to sell. Having one doesn't necessarily mean you have the other, and even if your business operates like a well-oiled machine, you'll have to make some changes if you want to get the highest possible price when you sell.

Typically, it takes between six to eighteen months to prepare a business for sale, depending on the size and complexity of the business. There are a couple of reasons this process takes so long. Primarily, you want both the financials and sales to look good, but you also want things operating in such a way that a prospective buyer feels they can take over your business with relatively little risk. The price a buyer offers you will reflect your business's future cash flows and the perceived risk to getting those cash flows. This means the lower the perceived risk, the higher the price you'll be offered.

Yet this is completely different from how successful businesses are operated. As a business owner, you're looking to maximize the future growth of your business, and very often, this means taking significant risks in order to do so. However, those risks have a meaningful impact in the way a future buyer perceives the certainty of your business's future. It takes time to restructure a business and make it less risky in the eyes of the buyer, but ultimately, it makes your business more valuable for that time period. For the first time, you need to shift from a long-term view to a short-term view.

When speaking with business owners who have successfully sold their companies, I've found they almost always took quite a while to get their business ready for sale. That often meant doing things such as cutting long term investments, increasing cash flow, increasing sales (sometimes at lower margins), or just creating a more focused business. Sometimes the changes these owners made felt more like sacrifices, because their decisions might have slowed future growth, and therefore, would have impacted the future of their business had they not sold it.

In Chapter 8, I discussed how entrepreneurs are constantly faced with choosing between making money today or making money in the future. It's a constant struggle, and as you prepare to sell your business, it will be necessary to consider this choice yet again and reevaluate it as if you were the buyer of your business.

One of the best things you can do when preparing to sell your business is to reappraise every aspect of your company from a buyer's point of view rather than your own. When doing this, be critical of all aspects of your business. Ask yourself, "If I were buying this business, what aspects of it would seem risky to me?" Ignore all the inside information you already know, because any prospective buyer will not have your knowledge about the business's operations. Once you identify those aspects a buyer might deem risky, you'll need to have explanations ready to counter them.

Also, you'll need to prepare for significant due diligence. The more you're being paid upfront for your business, the more thorough the due diligence process will be. If the buyer has more risk in the future and will be paying you over time, they won't have the same level of due diligence and risk aversion because your payment will be dependent upon your ability to hit certain milestones.

In Chapter 9, we discussed that it was necessary to create an idea of the types of companies you were looking to buy; things such as how much you were willing to pay upfront, how much you wanted to payout to the owner for their knowledge, and so on. When planning to sell your business, you need to ask yourself the exact opposite of those questions. What kind of transaction do you want to have? Are you going to want cash upfront, or over time? Are you willing to spend time transferring knowledge? If so, how much do you want to be paid for your help in transitioning the company? Create a similar list of things you are looking for in a buyer.

A lot of entrepreneurs underestimate the process of preparing their business for sale because of the affection they hold for it. They love their business; they built it and they're passionate about it. And it makes sense. After all, they've lived with the struggle and risk of failure for many years. This can make it very difficult to remove themselves from their business and see it with a fresh and neutral pair of eyes.

If you're feeling the same way, the best thing you can do is have a mental value of what your business is worth, and ask yourself if someone who didn't know anything about your company would be willing to pay that amount. Try to be objective when reviewing every part of the business, and when you find an area that seems to have risk, implement changes to make this area less risky or adjust your price realistically. It's up to you to create the highest possible value for your business because whoever buys it will certainly not have your conviction about its future success.

■■■■■

Vital Secret #16

Make yourself dispensable.

I was sitting with Ivan prior to dinner discussing his newly found freedom. Ivan built a large car-parts company and was preparing his business for sale when a purchaser came to his office and asked what he wanted for his company. Ivan wrote down the number he'd like as if all the work for transition was done. The buyer agreed without hesitation, and sent the millions of dollars the next week. No non-competes, no inventory review, no due diligence. There was almost no paperwork for the sale. Ivan agreed to stay on for a year and help operate the business. He kept the land and negotiated a long-term lease. Ask Ivan and he'll tell you he knows how unbelievably lucky he was. It, of course, doesn't hurt that Ivan has over the past few decades built a reputation as an honest and hard-nosed businessman. The buyer probably knew that Ivan's price was fair and that there wasn't much room to move. He also knew that Ivan had set up the firm in a way that allowed him a lot of free time to do the other things that were important in his life. In some ways Ivan had spent decades grooming his firm to operate without him.

▪▪▪▪

The more payment you want upfront, the more work you're going to have to do upfront. There is an inverse relationship between the value of a business and the owner's importance to it. Simply put, the more important you or any one person is to your business, the less valuable it will be to potential buyers. When a business is dependent upon the continuing work of one individual, that company can no longer be successful without that person. And in these situations, buyers aren't willing to pay the majority of the sale price upfront. If you're essential to your business's success, a buyer will want you around as long as possible, which means the majority of your payment will be dependent on your sticking around and achieving milestones down the road.

It's surprising how few people realize this when structuring their businesses. I touched on this area earlier, when we talked about the culture of your business and the people you hire, but this fact is especially true when selling your business. If you're the ultimate decision maker behind every operational issue in your business, there's a limit to how fast it can grow. After all, everything must be funneled through you, and for some people, the ability to control every aspect of their business is very important. Many entrepreneurs can leverage themselves, make the big decisions, and operate things quickly and efficiently. But because a prospective buyer isn't going to operate your business with you as the singular decision-maker, they have to be able to operate your business after you leave.

Unfortunately, many deals go awry simply because the person selling the business thinks the buyer will continue to operate things exactly as they did. This attitude often results in a breakdown of negotiations, where the buyer realizes they can't possibly pay the seller as much as they want because the seller would no longer have an incentive to work hard and make sure the business succeeds. Likewise, most buyers know that you cannot turn an entrepreneur into an employee. Very rarely can someone who has worked their whole lives for equity in a business be converted into someone who works for a salary and bonus.

■■■■

What Vital Secret #16 Should Mean to You

As I mentioned, the price you'll be offered for your business is going to reflect the value of the cash flows, discounted by the business's risks. Typically, the biggest single risk for any business is what happens once the key executives or owners leave. This is the first question the buyer is going to ask, which means you need to ask yourself what would happen to your business if you left.

Admittedly, this is the biggest conflict for most entrepreneurs. Through your persistence, intellect, and ability, your business succeeded and grew, but now it's your ability to be absent that will make it valuable. Not surprisingly, this challenge to the ego is a very hard one for most business owners. But as difficult as this may seem, it is essential. Let's consider a few examples.

Imagine that you are a barber and you own a barbershop. You have a nice little storefront with a few chairs, a barber pole out front, and low overhead because you're the only employee. Let's say you want to sell your business, but you don't know what it's worth. Unfortunately, it's worth almost nothing. In these situations, someone who comes in and takes over your barbershop is essentially buying your job. They're taking your position, since you're the only employee, which means they're basically paying you for the shop itself—not the business. The alternative is for that person to build their own shop, which may or may not be as cheap and easy as buying yours. Also, because you have a loyal client base that really loves getting their hair cut by you, what's going to happen when you're not there? Odds are many of your customers will stop coming when you leave. That reduces the value of your business to a new owner.

But let's say your barbershop has 10 barbers, and you've stopped cutting hair because you're managing the store full time. How would that business survive in your absence? It would probably do reasonably well, because you've employed a bunch of barbers who are doing the haircutting for you. They have their clients, and if you've treated your employees well, a potential buyer could come in and treat the barbers the same way without much turnover. So if the buyer continued to treat the business in a similar fashion, it would have a significant value. This business is worth more than 10 times what the other barbershop was worth, because you've gone from something that was valueless to something that's valuable.

This applies across the board, even in large companies. Consider Martha Stewart, for example. Her company, Martha Stewart Living Omnimedia, reflected Stewart's values and personality as an individual. By focusing on her ability to educate people about everything from throwing parties to decorating to cooking, Stewart was successful because she was the business's best ambassador. But once Stewart's reputation had been damaged by accusations of insider trading, her business suffered as well. The business was still a great business, but because it was so closely tied to Stewart herself, its value fell with her reputation. In fact, MSO stock dropped by 50 percent from the time the scandal broke until she was indicted. No matter what your business or its size, dependence on one person can have a significant impact on the value of a company, even one that's publicly traded.

■■■■

How to Make Vital Secret #16 Work for You

There are three things you should do to prepare your business for your departure, and it's essential to start this process well in advance. You cannot make yourself dispensable within a few weeks, so install this process months before you are ready to sell.

1. **Set up a decision-making process that keeps you informed but excludes you.**

   Before you sell your business, your employees need to be comfortable making everyday decisions without your input. This should be a gradual shift that takes place over time, and is very challenging for many businesses owners to make. Some successful businesses make this transition before their owners are ready to sell, and those that do operate on a day-to-day basis with the founders staying informed but not making many of the decisions.

   The goal of this transition is to remove menial decisions from your desk. This doesn't mean you shouldn't be involved in the strategic decisions of the business, but employees should progressively grow from making trivial decisions to larger ones as appropriate.

   Using the barbershop example, you might start by allowing employees to decide when additional supplies are needed, which cleaning service should be hired, and what kinds of ads are going to run and when. Of course, in a 10-person barber shop, there's a limited number of decisions you can pass down to employees. But if you owned 5 barbershops, each with 10 barbers, you might choose one person at each shop to be that location's decision maker, giving them the ability to make certain decisions without your involvement. As you implement this system, you'll begin reviewing their decisions rather than making them yourself.

   Buyers love it when a business's founder reviews operations rather than gets involved in them. This is because the buyer sees himself taking your position as the reviewer of the business—something much easier to do than making operational decisions. Obviously, you can't step too far away from your business, because you don't know that a transaction is actually going to happen. Regardless, there should be a balance between the decisions you make and the ones you review, and it's important that you set up this process.

2. Set up the business to operate successfully during an extended absence.

Before you sell the business, think of long vacations and extended absences as a test run. If you left for a one-month trip out of the country, and could not be reached during that time, would your business continue to operate successfully? The answer needs to be yes. If that's not possible in any way, shape, or form, then your business completely depends upon you. And if the business can't operate day-to-day without your presence, that's clearly an issue.

3. Set up an apprentice who will take your place in your absence.

If you're not able to leave your business for extended periods of time, this is how you should achieve that goal. Select an employee and mentor them on all aspects of your daily routine. This person should learn how you make decisions, how you do inventory, how you manage your balance sheet, and everything you do with regards to your business. The idea is that you're developing an apprentice who will be your eyes and ears while you are gone. Also, the buyer will see your right-hand man and able lieutenant as the ideal person to take over your business once you leave, or as someone who can educate them should you leave after you are paid. Again this reduces risk and increases the value of your business.

■■■■

Vital Secret #17

Sell when things are going great.

A great example of this comes from Kevin, whose company operated golf courses and country clubs around the country. Even though the company grew from 17 locations in the early '80s to over 300 by the new millennium, Kevin and his partners lost a significant part of their business's value by waiting too long to sell their business.

"We almost sold the business in 1998," explained Kevin. "We went through everything with an investment bank and had an offer, but it was a half cash, half stock offer from a REIT. When the offer was made, our chairman decided he didn't want half of the sale to be tied into this other company's stock. He also wanted to have a billion dollar transaction and we weren't quite there, but we were close. Because of this, we turned the offer down. We were certain that we would continue to grow."

"Over the next few years, we were unable to grow the business. We didn't have the capital necessary to expand and we were in some obligatory financial situations that impacted our cash flow. So pretty soon, we found ourselves in a situation where we needed to sell the business just to keep it viable. We went through the process again, but this time there were a lot of different suitors for the business and things were a lot less attractive, the market was more competitive, our revenue and profits were down."

The company was bought in early 2002 by a partnership of Goldman Sachs and Starwood Capital, which had some golf courses of its own through Starwood Hotels. "We would have done immensely better had we sold when things were going great," insists Kevin. "We saw the value of the business reduce by almost seventy percent during that time. What was almost a one billion dollar company in 1998 was reduced to less than three-hundred million dollars in 2002." Kevin and his partners were still able to sell their business, of course, but the profit they made could have been much more significant had they decided to sell when their business was at a high-water mark and there was only blue sky on the horizon.

In the United States, the lifespan of any great product or idea is 24 months. In fact, in many industries, it's less than that. If you do not constantly strive to enhance and improve your company and the service it offers, your business will suffer and possibly fail. The market in this country is so efficient that someone will always come along, copy your success, and do it better or cheaper than you within 24 months. Of course, this means that if you rest on your laurels and success, you will quickly fall behind. Success is always immediately copied.

This is one of the major shortcomings of many entrepreneurs. When things are going well, instead of acknowledging that it's eventually going to end, many business owners assume that it's going to continue forever. This is a dangerous attitude to have when you're operating a business and a deadly one when you want to sell it. This false sense of security means that you'll never be satisfied with any price you're offered because you expect your exponential growth to continue indefinitely. Unfortunately, it seldom does.

This kind of high growth continues only if you continue reinventing your business every 24 months. This could mean new enhancements to your existing products, new product ideas, or new improvements. Great examples of this can be seen in every area of service and every product on the market. The marketplace is constantly changing, and your potential customers and clients are always being offered something new, if not the same thing at a lesser price. In order to be successful, entrepreneurs need to constantly be vigilant and reinvent their business.

Andy Grove, Chairman of Intel, did an excellent job describing this pressure in his book, Only the Paranoid Survive. He spoke very eloquently of this continuous pressure, and it's just as true for independent businesses as for corporations. The moment you feel comfortable where you are at, your business is headed for trouble. Yet there is a positive aspect to this. If you sell your business when success is at a peak, everything you've developed and created is working as hard as possible. And if there's still some continued success in your business, then it's a perfect time to sell. If you wait, you'll have to come up with the next revision of your product or service to keep the success going. Otherwise you'll have a painful down cycle and you'll be forced to reinvent yourself. And many business owners don't have enough respect for how incredibly competitive and good the competition is in almost every industry.

■■■■

What Vital Secret #17 Should Mean to You

Business is cyclical, and every business goes through the same cycles our economy goes through. But there is another cycle that occurs; the life cycle of any product you invent, manage, or sell. As I mentioned, if you don't enhance your services and products and rejuvenate your business every 18 to 24 months, it will be hard for you to grow and thrive in all environments.

When selling your business, buyers will almost always extrapolate your most recent couple of years to estimate future earnings. And in doing so, they have a vast aversion to what's called "the hockey stick effect." This occurs when a business has had modest growth over last few years, but in estimating future earnings, the owner suddenly projects unreasonably huge growth going forward. The term hockey stick refers to what a graph would look like in these situations, and as a business owner, your business will get a much higher valuation at the top of the hockey stick than when it suddenly starts to go up (see Figure 11.1).

Buyers are weary of these extrapolations because usually the owner has very little justification to prove that the business will continue to grow at the same rate going forward. It's almost impossible for a business owner to explain why their company will have exponential growth in the future if it hasn't already experienced it in the last few years. Buyers also remain skeptical because if such rapid growth was truly possible, the owner would not be selling the business. If you knew today that your business could grow by 50 percent a year, how likely would you be to sell the business right now? If that kind of significant growth is going to happen, wouldn't you want to wait a few years before selling, rather than be paid less for that growth today?

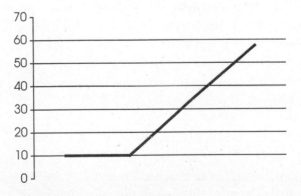

FIGURE 11.1. The "hockey-stick" projection.

You should note that the opposite of this is true, as well. If your business has grown 50 percent per year, it's certainly justifiable for you to sell. This is because you're in an ideal situation to get the most for your business. At times like these, you can tell prospective buyers, "I want to sell when things are great, which they are, and I deserve the highest possible premium and multiple for my successful company." But in that discussion it is also preferable to find a more practical reason. Some that were mentioned in the interviews we conducted are, "I'm getting older and want to move on," or, "I have worked so hard for so long that I want to take a breather," or "I love building companies but I don't love running them once they get to a certain size, so now is a great time to sell."

Unfortunately, many sellers become so unreasonably optimistic when business is good that it creates an impediment to a sale. Remember the 24 month rule: When things are going really great, someone will come along to challenge your business, and you'll seldom be as good as you anticipated. Because of this, there is a huge advantage to selling your business when things are going incredibly well, even if it means taking a modest discount or the buyer refuses to extrapolate continued high growth going forward.

There are two factors that determine the price you're going to get for your business. The first is the actual growth rate of your business and the second is the consistency of your growth over the past five years. All companies, public and private, have growth that ebbs and flows. And because growth is never consistent, revenue, which is very hard to disguise, ebbs and flows with your company's growth. The difference, however, between your business and a publicly traded company is that corporations have so many employees that they can reduce overhead when revenues aren't growing. But as a small, privately held company, you don't have that kind of flexibility. Buyers will simply look at your revenue growth to see how successful your business is, and they'll especially look at the last two years as an indicator of this. The more your revenue grows and faster the business grows, the better the valuation of your business will be.

For example, imagine you own an advertising agency. Your agency does $10 million a year in sales, and for the last couple of years you've been increasing sales by 20 percent per year. It's very easy to see a potential buyer come in, look at your business, and say, "I think we can expect to see 20 percent growth next year and the year after that." Their expectations would be based on your current growth, and they'd assume the trend would continue. You could also assume that the buyer might say, "Okay, if the rate of growth is 20 percent, then it will trim back after three years or so." Even if the buyer expected your company's growth to be between 10 percent and 15 percent after three years, you'd still be paid today for the future value of that growth. Even with reduced expectations, you'd be paid this amount above and beyond the current value of your agency.

But let's say you passed on the offer and waited a year to sell your advertising agency. If for some reason sales didn't grow by 20 percent the next year, but actually remained flat at $10 million, you'd have the same amount of sales. However, what would that same potential buyer put into their models looking forward? Well, they'd see today's earnings, so they'd pay the same for that. But since your sales are flat, the buyer might expect them to continue to stay flat, or maybe even go down in the future. So for the exact same business with the exact same current revenues and profits, it's likely that you would get less than you were offered a year ago. That's because today's value might imply that there's going to be diminishing sales going forward. What's worse, you can't possibly imply that the growth of 20 percent is going to return. Even if you were able to convince the buyer sales were going to increase again, it would be hard to get them to build that into their calculation when determining the price they're going to pay you.

This example clearly demonstrates why you need to plan for your sale before things are going well. Ideally, you should be negotiating with a buyer in the midst of a good cycle for your products or services. If you're a vendor or own a store, the best time to do this may be during the holidays. Likewise, if you sell and install air conditioners, you'd be smart to sell during the hot summer months. The idea is that you should negotiate with a buyer when business is good. Not only does the increased business excite the buyer, but it allows them to see that sales are great and that you have a thriving business.

The most important thing is to have a plan; to know when things look like they've turned a corner and business is growing. Once this happens, stay focused on growing your business, but start to put your exit plan in place and do everything necessary before you actually bring in a buyer.

How to Make Vital Secret #17 Work for You

1. **Meet at busy times.** The best way to show that things are going great is to make sure the buyer sees activity. In other words, make sure that you're meeting the buyer at a time and place for them to track this. It may be at your business or other location, but it should be at a time when business is busy. Whether your business is most active at a certain time of day, or season, or month, meet with the buyer when there is a lot going on. Also, make sure that plenty of things are happening at your office. One of the best ways to do this is to load the pipeline with activity in anticipation of meeting the buyers.

   If you own a retail store, offer special coupons or sales that coincide with the buyer's visit. Hand them out to customers or run ads a few weeks before the day your prospective buyer is going to be in the store. If you're in a different kind of business, be sure to create a sense of buzz and excitement among your employees and clients prior to the buyer's visit.

   Be upfront and honest with the buyer in these situations. Explain to them that you're running a sale, or that you just got a large order and are extremely busy. The main point here is that by having a lot of activity, the buyer will want to act more quickly and you'll increase the momentum of the transaction. If buyers get a sense that things are really happening, they'll have more incentive to act quickly.

2. **Manage your cash flow.** You need to start cutting back on long term investments in advance. This is because you need to be more fiscally conservative in advance of the sale, but still be able to show that you've made a lot of investments. In most businesses, modest reductions in spending on things such as technology, R&D, or even new chairs, will help your bottom line. Look for things that will have little impact on your operations and try to hold off purchasing those items. Doing so will increase your profits, and therefore, increase your valuation. These kinds of subtle changes can make a significant difference

to a buyer's valuation, especially if you're getting paid five or ten times your earnings. So look around for things your business can cut back on.

For example, in preparation to sell his business, one entrepreneur decided that he would have to approve any purchase over $5,000. He was able to cut his spending, which increased profits for 12 months prior to the sale.

3. **Be Realistic.** Look at the past, look at your competitors, and set realistic expectations of how your business will grow over time. In almost all instances any seller who misrepresents their past or is not realistic about the future will have a much tougher time selling their business and will probably have a challenge getting the price they want.

Remember that the future holds as much opportunity as the past and present. Not less, not more, but as much. If you truly believe the future will be exponentially better than the present, you're always better waiting until things improve before you sell.

Vital Secret #18

Reward the people that are important to the transaction.

"When we sold the business," explained Greg "there were a lot of great things we did to take care of our employees, but there were also a few mistakes made." Greg sold his insurance marketing company after running it with his wife for 15 years.

"When you're selling a business, there's a time to keep things quiet and close to the vest, and there comes a time to let your employees know. It's a difficult decision for any business owner, and I struggled with this question as well."

"We had two top salespeople, both of which were integrated into our management and had become close friends of mine. But for some reason, I

didn't trust them as much as I should have when negotiations were going on, so I held back from letting them know about the transaction. That decision came back to haunt me, because once the acquisition was announced, they both left the company within two months. Sadly, if they had been part of the transaction, I don't think it would have happened. To this day, I'm not sure what's the right time to tell employees, but I learned that not telling them doesn't work out."

I asked Greg what he could have done to save the situation. "Looking back, I probably should've written them each a check for fifty grand; something to say, 'Here's your share of the gains – your reward.' I was actually working to give them both equity ownership that would have far exceeded that amount, but it would have taken six months to get it set up. And because I handled things poorly with them initially, they weren't willing to wait it out."

But Greg did make some smart decisions when selling his business. "Fortunately, I gave my CFO ten percent of the gains. He was the third person in line to be compensated from the acquisition, after myself and my wife, who was my business partner. He was really instrumental not only in making the deal happen, but in the overall success of the business. And because we treated him well, he stuck around to the very end."

Greg also leveraged the benefits of working for the buyer to his advantage when convincing his employees to stay. "Other than the two salespeople, almost no one left. Our buyer was able to provide things like better health benefits, stock options in the parent company, and more vacation time, and made sure our employees knew this. So in the end, even those who didn't directly benefit from the acquisition still had some incentives to stick around."

■■■■■

What Vital Secret #18 Should Mean to You

As we discussed with acquisitions, one of the most important elements to a successful transaction is creating momentum. As a seller, one of the best ways to create this momentum is to provide incentives that encourage people to help make the transaction occur. This is not only true for your employees, but for any advisors you have, such as lawyers, accountants, or investment bankers that are involved in the sale of your business.

There are no secrets from money, and unfortunately, many entrepreneurs forget to reward the people who are important. Such a mistake can be costly. If these people have no incentive to see this transaction happen, what are your chances of motivating them to increase business and help the process? In the event your buyer asks to come in and meet your employees while doing their due diligence, the employees' attitudes will likely reflect their vested interest in the transaction. If they're not receiving an incentive, their attitudes may hurt your chances of selling. At the very least, the buyer may begin to believe that he will have to restructure the business.

Also, make sure you tell people about their incentives in advance. Once your employees realize that you're attempting to sell the business, they'll notice that you're less involved in the business's day-to-day operations. Because of this, it's best to be upfront and explain to the ones that mean the most that you are exploring this alternative. By offering incentives, you're letting employees know that you care about them and that this transaction will benefit them, as well.

The actual incentive may vary from employee to employee, and whether you're offering an extra three months of salary, extra vacation time, or stock in the company, it's important that you don't get carried away with incentives. I also suggest that you say little about the buyer, other than they love the business and want to come in and meet everyone. While you don't want your employees to expect huge changes, you want them to be excited when the buyer comes in, so that they share their passion and enthusiasm for the business.

It's especially important to remember the real creators of value for your business, and most of the time there are not many. It might be just one person, such as a lieutenant you've mentored, or three or four people who run different divisions of your business. Regardless, there are people in your business who have helped create its value and should be rewarded, even if they don't currently have a vested interest in the company. These individuals should have the most significant incentives of anyone you work with, and you should allocate a portion of the proceeds of the sale to your key personnel. Obviously, it's better if these individuals know what's happening prior to the transaction. It may seem like a good idea to surprise them afterwards, but if they don't know what's coming, they may not help you to make the transaction.

Finally, it's very important that as you have ongoing communications with the buyer, you will get a sense of who they see as an important part of the ongoing business. In many situations, you'll discuss this later in the transaction, and the buyer may ask for your guidance. If you've delegated decisions and mentored a lieutenant, as we discussed earlier, you'll know just who to suggest.

How to Make Vital Secret #18 Work for You

There are three things you need to keep in mind when it comes to incentives:

1. **Identify your most important employees.**

   It's not enough just to give incentives. You need to be sure you're giving the right incentives to the right people. Start off by identifying those people that are crucial to the success of the transaction. Those are the people who should have the most to gain from your success in selling the business (and who have the most potential for keeping it from happening).

2. **Create an appropriate compensation structure.**

   After identifying your key personnel, create a structure of incentives that appropriately reflects that person's contribution to making the sale of your business occur. Offer a modest bonus to all your employees, and increase the bonus depending on the importance of each employee. When selling our business, we placed our employees in different categories based on their importance to making the transaction occur. We then assigned different bonuses to each category of person.

3. **Work with professionals.**

   Finally, make sure you work with professionals to make the transaction happen. It's amazing how many business owners try to save money by doing things themselves. There are many lawyers who have consummated these kinds of transactions, and you're always better off spending the extra money on talent.

Remember that you get what you pay for, and while it might be a smart thing to save money while operating your business, you should get yourself the best help you can afford when selling it. So don't be pennywise and pound foolish. Experience counts and you probably don't have any in this area.

Just as the two brothers had to work together to get the highest price for their donkey, you need both a successful operation and the right preparation in order to sell your business for the highest price. A strong business with good operations will not sell itself, just as a superior salesman cannot get the best price for an inferior product.

Getting the highest price requires both salesmanship and a great product.

By preparing your business for sale and transitioning yourself from being involved in the business's operations to reviewing decisions, you'll be setting yourself up to earn not only a fair market value for your business, but the highest price possible.

Chapter TWELVE

The Negotiation

How to prepare for and what you must know

to complete the sale of your business.

Vital Secret #19

Deals either ripen or rot, so ABC (Always Be Closing).

The Price of Emotions

Masamba's House

Once there was an old and wise man named Masamba, who lived with his family in the heart of Africa. Masamba was loved by his community and had spent his whole life on the farm where he had raised his family. But as he grew old and his children left home, Masamba realized it was time to sell his land.

As Masamba prepared for his first interested buyer, he took a walk around his home. He remembered the joy and laughter his family had shared in these rooms, and felt saddened as he realized that he would soon be leaving these memories behind.

Soon a gentleman came to see Masamba's house and farm. Wanting to show the interested buyer all the wonderful aspects of his home, Masamba walked the man around his compound, telling him about its rich history. As they arrived at the first little building on his property, the man pointed to a hole in the wall.

"What happened there?" he asked.

"Ah, that's from my youngest son," Masamba explained. "He used to play in this shed, and that was his favorite place to hide his toys from his older brothers."

Seemingly uninterested, the man shook his head and walked on.

As they toured Masamba's house, the man seemed to take notice of small flaws and problems. "That oven looks kind of old," he said to Masamba.

"It is well-worn," admitted Masamba. "But that's because my wife used it quite often to make the best cakes and breads you'd ever taste. I can assure you it works quite well."

Next, Masamba showed the man his living room, which contained a large hearth. "There's quite a lot of soot in the fireplace," said the man. "And by the look of the black bricks around it, you haven't cleaned it in quite a while."

"Perhaps you're right," admitted Masamba. "Our family used it almost every night as we rested and relaxed together. I can't begin to count all the stories, jokes, and laughter that hearth has seen. I hope you enjoy it as much as my family has."

"That's not going to happen," explained the man. "I don't care about the fireplace, the old oven, or the hole in your wall, because I plan on tearing down all these buildings and constructing my own house. But despite these small problems, I'll give you 50,000 quacha for the house and land."

Masamba became incensed. "How dare you! Have you not listened to a word I said? I'm insulted, and I'm certainly not going to sell you my house just so you can tear it down. Get out of here!" And with that, Masamba threw the man out.

The next day, another interested gentleman came by to see Masamba's farm. And as with the day before, Masamba took the man on a tour of his land, pointing out the home's flaws to him and explaining the rich history behind his compound. Throughout the afternoon, Masamba shared the story of his son and the hole in the wall, the oven and his wife's wonderful cakes, and the great hospitality his hearth has seen.

But unlike the first gentleman, this man took an interest in Masamba's stories. "Tell me about your son," he said. "Did his older brothers pick on him?" He continued to take an interest in Masamba's life, talking to him at length about his wife and her cooking, as well as listening to some of the stories and jokes that Masamba remembered hearing in front of the fireplace.

Once Masamba was finished showing him the property, the man became quiet. "I must admit," he told Masamba, "I don't know how to put a value on such a wonderful home and so many great memories, but all I can afford to offer you is 40,000 quacha. I love your home, and I hope you don't consider this offer an insult, but this is all I can afford."

Masamba chuckled and patted the man on the back. "That's okay," he told the gentleman, "40,000 quacha is fine. I am just happy that you appreciate my home and see its history."

Shortly thereafter, Masamba packed his bags and took one last walk around his home. With a tear in his eye, he left the gentleman in his new home and wished him well.

Once Masamba left, the man made a telephone call to his friend who was a specialist in demolishing and rebuilding homes to tell him the good news.

The moral of the story: Emotions can be very expensive at the time of sale.

■■■■■

As the story about Masamba exemplifies, one of the most important things to realize when selling your business is that emotions are incredibly expensive. If you feel emotionally attached to your business as this process begins, you won't be objective about what the business is fully worth and the price you'll receive for it. Entrepreneurs who see their business in this light often take things personally and become offended. This mindset also makes it almost impossible for any prospective buyer to meet your standards; after all, no one is going to have the emotional attachment to it that you do.

When beginning to prepare your business for sale, this transition will undoubtedly be difficult. You've worked hard, long hours to make your business a success, and it's not a static, passive object that you can look at unemotionally. You'll immediately begin to think of all the pains and anxieties you had creating this business, as well as everything you had to overcome in order to make it valuable. In many ways, you may think of your business as your child—if you don't already.

Yet this mindset is exactly why so many transactions fall apart. Although you've poured your emotions into your business, nurturing it and taking care of it like a child in order to be successful, it is time to think differently. As you begin to prepare to sell your business, it is essential that you treat it like a house, a piece of property you want to dispose of.

Notice that I used the word house, not home. Masamba thought of his house as home, and his emotions cost him. So my suggestion is that you think of it much like a house you are selling for a good friend. It is an asset, but you are not attached to it.

The most important lesson is that you must keep your emotions out of the transaction. If you don't, you're going to end up just like Masamba. And remember that no matter who comes and buys your business, they will not have the emotional attachment to it that you do.

Before we discuss the Vital Secret for this chapter, I'd like to take a moment and address two concepts that are very important to remember before you begin the process of selling your business. First, you need to be practical and realistic, and second, changes will occur when negotiation starts in earnest.

1. Be practical and realistic.

This is as simple and straightforward as it sounds. When you're valuing the company, you have to be practical and realistic. This means that you must be able to look at the flaws in your business and measure its risks. If for some reason it is impossible for you to be objective, then you need to find someone who can give you an honest appraisal of the business. Taking the time to make a realistic assessment of your business means that you'll determine a fair and right price for the business, and your negotiations will come out fine. On the other hand, if you have unrealistic expectations for your business's worth, you'll probably find yourself marked-to-market. When that happens, the process becomes painful for everyone involved. An interested buyer will find his patience tested as he grinds you down to a reasonable price, while you continually face the reality and stress that your expectations were too high.

2. Changes occur when negotiation starts.

Also, you need to acknowledge that once negotiations begin for the sale price, the honeymoon is almost always over. As you begin showing interested buyers your business, you'll likely find yourself thinking this process will be easy and that things will go smoothly and quickly (just as I did). This is because initially, you're in a courting process where the prospective buyer is trying to convince you why you should sell your business to them. Yet the moment both parties commit to the transaction, you're going to find out a lot more about what the buyer is like. Once the process gets to the point where you initiate the sale, every buyer becomes much more conscious of their own self interests. Don't expect the honeymoon to last forever.

Vital Secret #19

Deals either ripen or rot, so ABC (Always Be Closing).

Jeff, who created a popular Hollywood sound studio with his partners, shared his experience with me. While owned by Jeff and his partners, his company won five Academy Awards and fifty Emmys by creating postproduction sound work for films and television shows.

"Rather than just making it known that we were looking for someone to buy our business," explained Jeff, "we realized that we needed some kind of sizzle in order to attract potential buyers. And in order to create this kind of buzz, I began negotiating with a virtual reality company. This included a commitment from some investment bankers to prepare to go public. We had an evaluation done of the business, began putting a presentation and book together for potential investors, and started down the path of taking the company public."

But rather than become listed on a stock exchange, Jeff's efforts paid off in a different manner. "During this time, the investment bankers learned that a competitor of ours was about to be purchased by Liberty Media, a huge media corporation responsible channels such as QVC, the Discovery Channel, and Encore, in addition to other media-related industries. Our bankers took advantage of the situation and positioned our company as a complement to our competitor. The result was that we were chased by Liberty Media because they were afraid we'd go public and gain a leg up on them."

Jeff went on to explain how negotiations unfolded. "When executives from Liberty Media came to visit our company, they told us they'd be in touch the next day. Well, a few days came and went, with no word from Liberty. I contacted my investment bankers, who told me to relax and that they were very busy with other deals. Not willing to wait, I created a reason to show up at their headquarters in hopes of getting a meeting. There'd been a company that I'd been interested in Denver, which was close to Liberty's offices in Eagleton, Colorado. So I made an appointment with the company and flew out to Denver, then had the investment bankers call Liberty Media to let them know I was in town on business in case they wanted to meet with me."

"Well," Jeff laughed, "at first the answer was no. But as soon as I got off the plane in Denver, I got a call from John Malone, the CEO of Liberty Media. 'Do you have time to stop by this afternoon?' he asked."

When Jeff met with Malone and other executives from Liberty Media, he found himself in a huge conference room overlooking nine private jets and listening to transactions of tens of millions of dollars treated as casual spending. But determined, Jeff was soon offered $125 million for the business—well over the $30 million dollar cap he and his partners expected based on his company's earnings.

"They called me at home on a Friday and wanted to fly in and see the business the following Monday," said Jeff. "I said that I was very excited about moving forward, but had yet to get an offer from them, or a letter of intent. I was told that I would get one on Monday and should plan to fly out to meet with the executives then."

But Monday came and went with no offer or letter of intent. Jeff knew both were essential if the deal was to move forward. An offer would give Jeff and his partners the dollar amount they needed to move forward, and a letter of intent would legally protect his company from being taken advantage of once Liberty Media had access to the company. Tuesday came and went with no word from Liberty. Finally on Wednesday, executives called Jeff.

"They were putting pressure on me to come out, but I stood my ground. I reminded them that I still hadn't gotten an offer or letter of intent, and told them that I wouldn't move ahead until I got those." Liberty Media promised Jeff that the documents would be waiting at his hotel once he arrived, so with some reluctance, Jeff flew out for the meeting. Sure enough, he found a packet waiting for him at the hotel with both documents.

Unfortunately, negotiations hit a difficult bump when Liberty Media decided to purchase yet another competing company. Jeff was forced to watch from the sidelines while Liberty Media moved to complete the purchases of his two competitors before buying his firm. And with executives from both of his competing firms now involved, Jeff's expectations for the sale suddenly dropped out from under him. "Everything went back to square one," he explained, "because our competitors' deals impacted the terms of our deal."

As negotiations progressed, Jeff was told that he would become president of the new division being created by these three companies. Eventually, executives at Liberty Media decided that Jeff would have a senior position in the division, but would report to another executive involved. Frustrated, Jeff accepted the change because of his willingness to complete the deal, and forged ahead.

Just when things looked to be almost complete, Liberty Media told Jeff and his partners that they changed their minds and intended to bow out of the acquisition. After some discussion, Liberty Media agreed to move ahead, *but insisted Jeff change the valuation of his company and reform the company's planned business model. To make matters worse, Liberty Media reduced their purchase price for the company to $50 million. By this time, negotiations had been ongoing for well over a year, and Jeff was completely devastated. Realizing the fundamental terms of the offer were being changed, Jeff contacted a law firm and discussed the possibility of suing Liberty Media for breaking their letter of intent.*

Yet Jeff never went to court. Although he and his partners didn't threaten executives at Liberty Media with the lawsuit, the company heard about their plans and upped the price they were willing to pay for Jeff's firm. In the end, Jeff and his partners sold the company for $90 million, well above the $50 million that Liberty Media insisted they pay, but also far less than the $125 million first offered for the company.

If nothing else, Jeff's tale is a testament to dedication and momentum. Throughout his ordeal, Jeff endured mock meetings to get his foot in the door, the involvement of two of his competitors, impatient partners, slow contracts, intimidating executives, and the possibility of a lawsuit. Yet when all was said and done, the transaction was completed. The bigger the transaction price, the bigger the hurdles you'll need to overcome.

■■■■■

Every acquisition needs an immense amount of momentum in order to be completed. My mentor, who successfully created and sold three businesses, always said, "In order to actually make an acquisition happen, you need to get to a point of white heat." In other words, he meant that everyone involved in the transaction must be completely and totally focused on making it happen. And in order to rally everyone's attention and energy to this task, you need to set up a process that will keep building momentum until you reach a completed transaction.

This is essential because both the buyer and seller are running their respective businesses, and without a process, things are left unattended and incomplete. This eventually leads to the transaction falling apart. More than anything, the key to this secret is to be focused on building momentum and never taking your focus off the sale of your business.

Also, I've found that most people who have successfully sold their business, especially those who accomplished significant sales at high prices, have used agents. These individuals were smart enough to understand that they could not do it all themselves and used a professional consultant to help them through the process. More importantly, they recognized the need for an impartial agent during the transaction. Just like when you're selling a home, you need someone who does not have a vested interest in it to recognize a fair offer and terms rather than hold out for unreasonable expectations.

So if the person who's helping you and doing the negotiation on your behalf has a single, clear agenda, which is to sell your business, and they'll be compensated for completing that transaction, they're going to make sure the process continually moves forward. They also won't be insulted when a potential buyer makes an offer that doesn't work, because they'll be focused on the big picture—completing a sale.

Admittedly, there are a handful of people who choose to sell their home themselves and do it successfully, but most of us don't have the emotional makeup to remain detached and to distance ourselves from our business in order to not be insulted or offended.

■■■■

What Vital Secret #19 Should Mean to You

As I mentioned, one of the biggest surprises that occurs when the courting process for your business is over and negotiations begin is how quickly the tone and structure of the transaction changes. Most of the time, the seller continues to think of himself as being in the selling and convincing stage, while the buyer's mindset has shifted from being interested in the business to now realizing that he is parting with his money.

This shift significantly changes the dynamics of the relationship between the buyer and seller because you go from being on the same side of the desk to being on opposite sides. All of a sudden, the buyer decides to no longer look at the positive aspects of your business and its potential opportunity. Instead, he focuses primarily on its potential problems and risks.

As an example, consider the house analogy. Let's say a prospective buyer has come to look at your vacation house that you're selling. When he first sees it, he's going to notice all the great things about it—the pool in the back yard, the beautiful picture windows, the two-car garage, and Japanese garden. Naturally, people would see these things and be convinced that the house is fantastic. But as the interested buyer comes back to see the house a second and third time, that impression begins to fade as he becomes more critical.

Once the buyer decides he'd like to make an offer on the house, he truly becomes quite critical of its flaws. He'll start to notice that those beautiful picture windows let in a draft, or that there's a crack in the pool and it needs to be replaced. He may notice that the automatic garage door opener doesn't work every time the button on the remote control is pushed. Just because you're accustomed to a crack in the pool, or a temperamental garage door opener, doesn't mean the buyer isn't going to be concerned about these things. In these situations, you want to be able to give them an answer that will make them feel better. "I've noticed that," you may say about the garage door opener, "and we've had it checked. There's a wiring problem, and we're having that replaced next week."

Smart buyers will even bring their own inspector to make sure that these kinds of negatives aren't serious. Just as you'd have an inspector check out a house before you buy it, a buyer may have someone do the same thing to your business. Just as a homeowner needs to address a buyer's concerns about a sticky garage door opener, you need to be able to address concerns about your business. You're a huge component of your business, and your expertise and know how is necessary in order for a buyer and their consultants to understand your business. This means that you're going to have to sit there and watch as someone points out these flaws and problems, whether it's a crack in the swimming pool, a sticky garage door opener, or in the case of your business, an outdated manufacturing machine that needs new parts.

Realize that all those little things you've been meaning to do and have put off will come out. This is why the previous chapter focused on preparing your business for sale. Prior to even bringing in a potential buyer, it's important that you prepare your business as much as possible for that level of investigation and scrutiny. Businesses that have prepared themselves for sale by making improvements and minor fixes almost always end up getting a better price than those that don't. After all, when you sell a house, what's the easiest way to improve its appearance? By giving it a new coat of paint and making sure it's clean and tidy. By taking the time to make your business appear better, you're going to have a higher level of interest and probably receive a higher price. Just as with houses, initial impressions are important, so make sure you've done everything you can.

Of course, no amount of preparation is going to cover every possible issue or unforeseen problem. No matter how much you prepare, you cannot avoid this shift in the buyer's mentality nor can you stop them from seeing the negatives. No matter how critical they become, remember that your single focus is to complete the transaction. Things are going be brought up that you never thought of as problems, and when that happens, you need to acknowledge and accept them: then you need to come back with a solution. The more you can negate the risks the buyer sees in your business, the better. This is true whether you agree that their problems truly need to be addressed, or whether you feel that they are concerned about something very minor and trivial. At the end of the day, you've got to keep the buyer interested in completing the transaction; this means they must continually see this as a huge opportunity to make money with their investment, and you have to remove as much risk as possible. Address their concerns no matter what to keep the momentum moving.

Also, most concerns that a buyer will bring to the table reflect one of two issues. Either the buyer is worried that this issue will impede the future success of the business, or they see this issue as a risk because they don't understand it. Any issue you're likely to hear falls into one of those two categories, and by realizing which of these apply to a buyer's concern, you'll know how to best address the issue. Keep these two issues in mind, and you'll be able to keep moving forward and always be closing.

There's a handful of other things this secret should mean to you:

1. Keep your ego in check.

This applies at both extremes. Not only should you avoid bragging or emphasizing your importance to the business, but you should stand up for yourself and remember that you are an equal party in negotiations. It may be tough for you not to talk about how your business succeeded because of you, or how you were the one who recognized the need for a product improvement, but remember that the more a buyer believes you're solely responsible for the success of your business, the less valuable it will be. As I emphasized in the previous chapter, there is an inverse relationship between your importance to a business and the value of it, so keep your ego in check.

This is also important because buyers will criticize some aspects of your business that you personally thought of. For example, when selling a house, you may have had dark carpet installed years ago, and the buyer may think it's ugly. At the time it was installed, however, it may have been very popular. But if your ego's invested, you may disagree and insist that it's a perfectly fine carpet. When that happens problems are created.

Just as your personal opinions are completely irrelevant when a person is buying a house from you, the same applies to selling your business. A prospective buyer is going to believe what they want, and you will be unable to change their mind. So share your insights with buyers when issues arise, but remember that ultimately, it's their choice.

2. Work with agents.

Just as a smart buyer will get an independent assessment of your business, you should also hire talented professionals who know how to get deals done. Whether it's a lawyer, an investment banker, or even an experienced friend, don't be afraid to spend money on their expertise. It is surprising just how many will try to handle their own transaction. Others try to hire the cheapest middleman they can find, rather than the best person they can afford. So make sure the experts you have on your team have done these kinds of transactions several times. Otherwise, this mistake could cost you a fortune.

When choosing professionals to assist you, make sure the individuals aren't going to impede the transaction. The company acquiring you will undoubtedly have done this before and will have a lawyer reviewing documents, so you need one as well. Yet the challenge in finding a lawyer is making sure they understand your goal—to make a transaction occur. I emphasize this because by their nature, lawyers are paid for conflict. The more they debate, the more conflict there is, the more they're paid. Whereas if you make it clear to the attorney that you're going to pay them for completing the transaction, he'll have a vested interest in seeing the outcome occur.

How to Make Vital Secret #19 Work for You

There are four things you need to do in order to always be closing: get an honest valuation of your business, establish a *death march*, keep your sense of humor, and get when you give. To better explain, let's discuss each in detail.

1. **Get an honest valuation of your business before you start the negotiation process.**

    As I've discussed, one of the most important things you can do is have an honest appraisal of your business, and that appraisal should address both its potential value and potential risk.

    When selling a house, many people have several agents look at it and give their assessment of its worth and price. You'd also be smart to look at the market, comparing houses similar to yours, and seeing what they are selling for. Doing so gauges you within the real estate market, and the same thing should be done with your business. If you've done your homework, you'll have some idea of the business's worth already, so when meeting with agents, you'll know who's close to a fair market price.

2. **Establish a "death march."**

    The term "death march," refers to the French Foreign Legion. When stationed in North Africa, these soldiers would regularly have to march through the desert to get from one fortress to another. Because of this, they would stop at an oasis at every opportunity to rest, yet many soldiers died during these long, difficult hikes. The soldiers who made it to their destination were the ones who stayed motivated by focusing on the next oasis and their final destination.

The same mindset applies to you when selling your business. It's important that you not get overwhelmed by an ever-growing laundry list of issues, changes, and activities that have to happen in order to complete the deal. When you are negotiating, you need to keep focused and motivated just like soldiers marching through the desert—one step at a time.

When selling our business, we had regular meetings with the buyer to set milestones that had to be met before the next meeting. This allowed us to know what everyone was doing each step of the way, and as a result, there was never a time where every person involved on both the buyer's side and the seller's side didn't have something to do.

Why is this important? Well, not only does it get things done, but it keeps people's attention focused on the transaction. At first, you may start with weekly meetings, and then move to meet twice a week as things progress. The meetings should get closer together as you get closer to completing the transaction. But without a doubt, you should never go more than a week without having a conference call or meeting.

If you let too much time pass between meetings, everyone will inevitably regress to their day-to-day jobs. So you've got to keep focused on maintaining positive momentum, and the only way that's going to happen is to have consistent and ongoing meetings.

3. Keep your sense of humor.

As this process moves along, there will undoubtedly be times of huge tension and frustration. When you feel this way, the single most important thing you can do is find a way to diffuse your anger and frustration. These emotions should never come out in the transaction itself because they will cost you. Either you'll annoy the buyer and they'll change their offer, or they'll adjust one of their terms because of your emotional reaction to an issue.

Staying loose is essential, and a great example of this is former president Bill Clinton. No matter what happened, be it Whitewater, the Lewinsky scandal, or other trying events, he never got ruffled in any situation. I'm not condoning Clinton's morals or actions that might have created these issues, but his ability to handle these difficult situations. Whenever something arose that he wasn't comfortable with, Clinton always said, "Let me get back to you," or he smiled and defused tense situations. You should do the same. Whenever you feel your emotions surging, just say, "Let me look into that and get back to you." When you clearly start to feel frustrated, make a point of checking out of the situation. Do not react, because all you will do is create problems.

A good way to keep your sense of humor is to have someone you can vent to. Whether it's your spouse, good friend, or someone else, you need someone you can vent to and get empathy from. It's not necessary that they give you good advice, because you should be getting that from the professionals you've hired, but you do need someone you can lean on.

My wife was the person I spoke with, and she was always sympathetic towards me. She was my advocate and friend throughout the whole trying ordeal, and when it felt like I was venting to her too much, I would go to one of my lifelong friends. At first I needed to blow off some steam once a week, but as things progressed and became more stressful, it happened almost daily. I'm sure my frustration had a lot to do with the size of the transaction we were making, but even on a smaller deal, you're going to have regular doses of tension. So whomever you vent to, they need to remind you of the big picture—that this is all about selling your business.

Sometimes when you're in the midst of battle, it's hard to keep your cool, so have someone to help keep things in perspective.

4. Get when you give.

This means that when the buyer asks you to make a concession in the terms of the deal, you should always ask for a concession in return. The concession you ask for does not need to be in the same area, or even on the same topic, but you should ask for it without fail.

During negotiations, both you and the buyer are going to have a collection of issues that are important to you. Whether it's how much they're going to pay you for your business, or the amount they're going to pay upfront, there will be a myriad of things you're going to disagree on. Because of this, you need to make sure that you have a plan for how to address this.

For example, if the buyer wants to give you a lower price because he believes your machinery is old, you can say you'll accept less but you want more cash up front. This kind of give-and-take establishes certain expectations, so whenever the buyer comes to you to resolve an issue, he'll know that you are going to want him to resolve an issue as well. This becomes extremely helpful; every time something is brought up, two issues are resolved.

To see that this happens, I strongly suggest you create a list of dispute issues, and that you prioritize them on a scale of one to five; one being trivial and five being a strike item for you. You should also do the same thing from their perspective, which will give you insight into their dispute issues.

We did this ourselves, and started out with a list of about 250 contentious items. Of course, it looked insurmountable when we were starting, but whenever there was a dispute item, we would add it to our list, and then rank how important it was to us, and how important it was to them. It was extremely helpful, because when they wanted us to give on an issue that was important to them, my partners and I knew we could come back with something that was equally important to us. In fact, whenever possible, we asked them to give on an issue that we knew was relatively trivial to them but important to us. At the same time, when they asked us to give on an issue, we tried to do so for things that were important to them, but trivial to us. This was perhaps the smartest thing we did during negotiations, because it allowed us to get the most of what we wanted with minimal conflict.

So make sure you have a spreadsheet with all the dispute items, and keep it internal. Don't allow the buyer to see it, and continue to add to it as things progress. You may find you're willing to give on trivial things that are important to the buyer. Make a point of telling yourself, "I know this is important to them, even though it's trivial to me. So if I give them this, I'm going to get something that's important to me." This is one of the biggest secrets of negotiation, yet it's surprising how few buyers and sellers actually do this. If you take advantage of this information, you may find that your buyer gives things up without considering their importance to you.

Just as Masamba was unprepared and emotional when it came time to sell his house, you run the risk of losing money if you act the same way. It's essential that you not only detach yourself emotionally from your business as you negotiate, but that you hire professionals, evaluate your business, maintain momentum, and keep your sense of humor as you sell your business. Don't let your ego become an expensive distraction.

Emotions can be very expensive at the time of sale.

By keeping your emotions and ego in check, as well as having professional help during negotiations, you get more of what you want and give up less during the sale.

Chapter THIRTEEN

Letting Go

What you will experience when you are done.

Vital Secret #20

Be gracious and smile when you leave.

Fortune

Nakia's Luck

There once was a farmer named Nakia who lived with his family in a small African village. He was a superstitious man, and whenever something happened, he looked to the event as a sign of fate.

Nakia's farm had many types of animals, and one day, while feeding his donkeys, he noticed that one was missing. Fearing that the donkey had run off, Nakia went to see the village witch doctor for advice.

"One of my donkeys has disappeared," Nakia told the witch doctor. "Is this a bad omen of things to come?"

Nodding his head, the witch doctor calmly replied, "Good, bad, who knows? Only time will tell."

Confused, Nakia went home and returned to his farming. The next day, as Nakia went to feed his animals, he saw that the donkey had returned and that another donkey had followed the animal home. Excited, he rushed to see the witch doctor.

"My donkey has come back," Nakia explained to the witch doctor, "and has brought another donkey with him. Is this a sign of great things to come?"

Again, the witch doctor replied, "Good, bad, who knows? Only time will tell."

Nakia returned home, and the next day his son took the new donkey for a ride. Not used to carrying humans, the donkey threw Nakia's son off its back, breaking the boy's leg. Upset, Nakia went yet again to see the witch doctor.

"My son has broken his leg trying to ride the new donkey," Nakia explained. "What can this mean? Could this be a truly bad omen?"

"Good, bad, who knows?" said the witch doctor again. "Only time will tell."

Nakia returned home and took care of his injured son. The next day, the chief of the village announced that all of the young men in the village would be sent into battle against one of the neighboring tribes. As the young men left that afternoon, Nakia's son stayed behind, unable to fight because of his broken leg.

The following day, the village learned that there had been no survivors from the terrible battle, and that all of the young men in the village had been captured or died fighting.

The moral of the story: You'll never know the true nature of your fortune until it has passed.

For most entrepreneurs, the period after they sell their business is one of the most confusing times of their business lives. Throughout the interviews I conducted for this book, and my experience managing money for entrepreneurs who sold their companies, I've seen many people suffer a loss of identity.

It's not surprising, given that successful business owners pour their heart and soul into building a company. If you've done the same, you understand. The business becomes not only who you are but is also a reflection of you. Often, your friends and acquaintances view you as inseparable from your company. This strong identity is built over years, and then once the business is sold, it's suddenly gone. Only afterwards do many entrepreneurs realize how unhealthy this can be. Almost every person we interviewed used the phrase "it's like having a death in the family" after they described the ecstasy of seeing their life's work rewarded.

To demonstrate, let me share with you my own experience regarding this detachment.

Once my partners and I sold Centurion Capital, I stayed on with the business for a while. Initially, I thought that things would remain much the way they'd always been, only with a new name. I expected the business to operate the same way it had in the past, with the exception of some modest changes. I also knew that instead of reporting to my own board of directors, I'd now be reporting to some senior management at GE Financial, but other than that, not much would be different. GE had offered me a multiyear contract, which paid me well, so I felt that the company wanted me to stay and continue to do everything I'd done to make the company successful.

I was very excited to run my old company with the GE brand behind me, not to mention the company's resources. But as time passed, I realized that the fit was not particularly good.

After a few months, it became obvious to me that my relationship with my old company might not work out. I was becoming frustrated with the speed at which things happened. I sensed that GE was frustrated with my need to get things done in a hurry and immediately respond to issues as they came up.

This is not to say one way of working is preferable over the other. GE had a well-established and successful way of doing things, as did I. But in the end, the biggest conflict was the fact that I had led the business for so many years that it wouldn't work for the employees for me to stay. After all, the one certainty about this situation was that GE was not going to stop doing all the things that had made them successful. Had it not been the company I'd helped to build it might have worked out differently, but it was hard for me to be distanced from it.

I went home one day knowing that the time had come for me to make a decision. Was I in or was I out? I didn't want to be unfair to GE nor to the company I'd sold to them. That night, my wife and I had a long discussion, and it was a tough decision. I had a very nice contract with GE Private Asset Management that basically involved no risk on my part. My job was to show up and do what I'd always done with some modest changes, but I also knew there was little chance of me being happy with the job. As my wife explained, no money in the world or secure contract was as important as my happiness, and she said I should go on to the next chapter of my life.

I'd spent 10 years making my business successful, and it was finally time to start something new. I reminded myself that I was still a young guy with a whole future ahead of me. There would soon be new and exciting things to do.

So I handed in my resignation, and GE Private Asset Management and I parted ways very amicably. It was really awkward for me, but at the same time, fantastic. As I mentioned before, employees cried and came and thanked me for my guidance and mentoring, yet I knew leaving at that time was the right thing to do.

Of course, you're probably assuming that as soon as I left, I went on a great vacation and relaxed, shopping and spending my newfound wealth. Unfortunately, nothing is further from the truth. The day I left GE Private Asset Management, I began working on a new book and getting my hands into various new ventures.

So here I was, immediately working fourteen hours a day, because I feared that if I didn't get something happening immediately, all my contacts and relationships would disappear. I even felt compelled to keep my mind sharp, because I was concerned that it would get soft, and that my brain would no longer work at the same level of intensity it had been used to. I'm not the only one; this is something I have heard from many business owners who sold their company. How do you describe who you are when for years you've been the president of something? One entrepreneur, Ron, felt great about selling his company. Then one day he drove past the building he used to work at and noticed his name was no longer on the side of the building. The new name was up, and he felt a surge of emotion looking at the building. Another entrepreneur, Mike, would automatically wake up and find himself preparing to go to his office. One day he even found himself driving toward his office when he realized he no longer worked there. You don't just stop years of habit immediately.

Throughout this time, I frustrated my wife immensely, as well as myself. I had lots of sleepless nights—jarring awake in a cold sweat, wondering what I was doing, what my life was about, and what I was trying to accomplish. I was completely lost. I was contractually obligated to stay out of the asset management business, but every few days I'd get a call from an old employee asking how I was doing. I'd been the president of Centurion Capital and GE Private Asset Management, and all of a sudden, I was an unemployed guy with a few million dollars in my bank account. Overnight, I'd lost my identity. I didn't know how to describe who I was or what I did.

This went on for several months, but Jen, my wife, remained incredibly patient. "You've spent the last 10 years married to your company," she said to me, "and all of a sudden it's not any part of who you are. It's going to take time for you to be okay."

Looking back, I'm grateful that I never put any real money into any of the ventures I was considering at the time. The one piece of advice I'd heard from people who had similar levels of success was: "Don't put your money into anything for at least 12 months." I heeded that advice, mainly because I'd heard nightmares of people losing everything by jumping straight into a new business right after their success. I wasn't arrogant enough to believe that I had a magic key to making a fortune. And quite frankly, I spent a lot of time looking for good opportunities, but none of these turned out to be as promising as I'd hoped.

During this period, I was also dealing with conflicted feelings about my own company. I was constantly getting updates about the business, and while I wanted it to be successful, the ugliest and most insecure part of me hoped that it would miss me in some way. These feelings were a lot like what happens after a relationship ends; you're hurt, but you also want to be the first one to go out and start dating again. Needless to say, my life was very awkward during those first few months.

As time passed, I slowly started to become comfortable with my new freedom. I no longer felt uncomfortable driving around in the middle of the day without a suit. Granted, it was initially an awkward experience for someone who was used to working from 6:30 a.m. in the morning until 6:00 p.m. everyday. Yet here I was, walking around in jeans and a t-shirt, having coffee with potential business associates.

Like everything else, time passed and I got used to my new freedom. I've always prided myself on being an adaptable person, but I'm surprised how long it took me to become comfortable with my new situation. Yet, by the time a year had passed, it was inconceivable for me to go back to my former environment. Like Nakia, I learned just how hard it is to recognize good fortune as it's happening.

I remember on my one-year anniversary, thinking how happy I was that I'd left and what a great a place I was in. I'd started a new company that was looking pretty solid, and I was on track with the next phase of my life. But it took me a year to really appreciate my good fortune.

Vital Secret #20

Be gracious and smile when you leave.

We've already mentioned Jeff, who sold his postproduction sound studio to Liberty Media. Given Jeff's numerous difficulties when it came time to sell his business, he also provided some helpful insights into leaving your business.

"Once the sale was said and done, I had an agreement to stay through the end of the year. It was my responsibility to oversee the integration of the business, everything from IT to accounting and personnel. That was a very cold period for me and everyone involved, because of the way the deal had gone. So here I was, in our huge offices with only twelve other people who were still around from the hundreds of employees we had."

Jeff admits it was a difficult time for him. "In fact, my partners, who were both sound experts, had gone over to Liberty to work in the new division. It was a cold feeling. I was exhausted, I was getting gray hairs, and I was literally the only one left. It quickly became, 'What's the point?' My two existing businesses were in other states, and I was by myself."

As part of the deal, Jeff had negotiated to stay in his existing offices for an additional year. Continuing to run his other businesses, Jeff moved a few of his employees from Florida and continued to work alongside Liberty Media employees who were now working in his former business. He had these huge offices with no people in them. It felt cavernous and lonely.

"At the end of the year, we loaded up everything we were able to take with us—computers, furniture, chairs, anything that was ours—and moved to our new offices in Burbank. It was so sad," he admitted. "It was a very difficult departure."

As you can see, Jeff stayed in his old offices because he wanted to take advantage of his contract. But because the sale of his company had been so difficult, he paid an emotional price for staying around too long and for leaving on such bad terms.

What Vital Secret #20 Should Mean to You

When it comes to leaving your business after it's sold, there are a few ways things can play out. Typically, there are three kinds of departures:

the prearranged departure, the ambiguous departure, and the unintended departure. In order to understand each of these, let's take a look at them individually, as well as when each method works, and when it doesn't.

1. Prearranged Departure.

This is when the buyer and seller agree to a very short handover, after which the seller leaves. For example, let's say Steve is a mortgage broker whose business sells mortgages to homeowners, and that he has sold his business to ABC Bank. In this situation, the bank is simply buying Steve's list of clients, which means that once he hands over his list of clients, there's really nothing left for him to do. As a result, Steve hands over his list of clients, along with the business, he gets his check for the sale of the business, and off he goes.

When It Works

This is the cleanest way of organizing a departure, because everyone knows upfront that there will be no ongoing relationship, which also means that there are no issues to manage after the transaction. Both the buyer and the seller know how the sale will play out and have incentives to make things go smoothly. This works extremely well when the seller helps to accommodate all of the buyers' needs, as well as when the buyer has a good understanding of the seller's business. In Steve's case, it works extremely well if ABC Bank's client list resembles Steve's own.

When It Doesn't

This doesn't work well when the buyer has a completely different client base than the seller's and needs ongoing help with transitioning the business. In these situations, if the seller has been told that he is not needed, he'll be very hard to reach.

In this kind of transaction, the seller has very little time to adjust. They literally sell their company, and they're gone. This means you go from being involved to leaving almost immediately. It's a lot more abrupt, and you'll need to prepare yourself for that eventuality.

Mike has experienced this kind of rapid exit first hand. As a young software programmer, Mike founded a data systems company with his brother at the age of twenty. After designing workforce management software, the business shifted to an Internet model in 1999. The divisions of his business were sold to Microsoft and ADT.

"When I sold the company to ADT," explained Mike, "the transaction took three days. I literally had my box of personal items in my hands and was out the door in three days."

Even though Mike had prepared for his departure, it was still difficult. "I didn't have the panic that many entrepreneurs have, that kind of pain in your gut as you think 'What am I going to do now?' I was mentally ready for my exit, because I'd been planning and preparing for it. But still, things happened so quickly that I didn't have time to realize some of the feelings I was about to have once I was out the door."

Mike also echoed the sentiment that many entrepreneurs shared with me. "Selling my business felt like a death in the family. There were feelings of elation and joy, because your baby's going on without you, but you're also depressed, because you've worked so hard to build this organization, and in my case, it was gone within three days."

2. Ambiguous Departure.

This is when the buyer tells the seller that he wants him to stay, but actually doesn't. In some cases, this occurs because the buyer thinks that the seller will only agree to sell if he has an ongoing role in the business. Regardless of whether the cause is the seller's ego or that he truly loves the company, the buyer will tell the seller what he wants to hear, despite having no intention of keeping him on board.

There are ways to tell if this is occurring. You can tell if this is going to happen to you if the buyer offers you a consulting agreement rather than an employment contract, or they offer an employee position that removes all effective operating controls over the business. This is not to say that you shouldn't go ahead with the transaction when this happens, but you'll need to be prepared for what's going to happen. If you find yourself in this situation, keep it in mind as you negotiate the sale.

When It Works

It works when the seller has complete awareness of what is occurring and factors that into their decisions. It also works if the buyer has legitimate needs for consulting from the seller. For example, let's say Steve knows that he's not needed, and that the seller is offering him a consulting position because they think it matters to him. As a result, Steve wisely places very little value on the consulting agreement and makes sure that he gets all the money he needs upfront. Of course, another possibility is that the buyer actually does need Steve and is responsive to his needs. In this situation they'd actually take his advice, which is the scenario that everyone assumes will happen.

When It Doesn't

This type of structure seldom works well for the seller unless they're prepared for it. Often, the entrepreneur gets a vague employee contract, and they'll adjust their price to reflect the expected ongoing revenue stream. Yet in many of these situations, the entrepreneur walks away because he's frustrated working in a zero-control position.

For example, let's say Steve sells to ABC Bank, and they tell him he's an important part of the business. They offer Steve a three-year consulting contract to provide advice and guidance as clients are transitioned over. Steve honestly believes he's going to be making nice consulting income over the next three years, so he isn't aggressive on his sell price. After the first couple of months, they have an ongoing barrage of problems, and whenever Steve contacts ABC to sort things out, they don't return his phone calls. Steve still sees his former employees, but they now report to someone else at the bank, and he feels completely powerless. So being a man of principle, Steve gets frustrated and walks away from his consulting contract. This is a case I've heard several times, and usually the seller's frustrations were because they didn't understand the buyer's motivations.

3. Unintended Departure.

This is when both parties want the seller to remain. The buyer wants the company to continue to operate the way it has in the past, but they'd like some additional reporting, so they want you to run the company. In this instance, you'll know that this is the case when everyone in the business is hired to be employees of the buyer. You'll also be given additional responsibilities, to keep the parent company informed. These are some of the best signs that things are going to stay almost the same as before.

In Steve's case, this could be when ABC Bank wants Steve's company to become a regional office. They'll change the name of his business to reflect the bank, but Steve will continue running it and be trained to work with the bank.

When It Works

This works extremely well when the seller is able to become a reporting employee for the buyer. This is not all that common, because entrepreneurs typically start a company because they don't like being an employee for someone else. This also works well when the buyer allows the company it acquired to operate in a similar fashion to the way it did in the past.

When It Doesn't

This doesn't work when the seller is incapable of being an employee for another company and partnering with another company. Another reason this may not work is when the buyer aggressively implements changes that cause friction between the buyer and seller.

■■■■■

In general, many sellers overestimate their importance to their business, while many buyers underestimate and underutilize the knowledge of the seller. This is why so many acquisitions are initially cumbersome for both parties. Because of this, it's healthy to have an open dialogue and to keep your ego in check when discussing the transaction. Do your best to understand what the buyer would like to have happen with you, and let it be clearly known that you have no personally vested interest in the business once it's sold. By letting the seller know you're flexible with whatever role they want you to play, they'll be able to be reasonably honest with you.

Personally, my partners and I were very candid with GE Financial. We explained to GE that we were completely happy to walk away from our business if that's what they wanted. We were open and flexible to whatever their intentions were with us as future employees.

As it turned out, Bob was their consultant, I worked for them for about a year, and Jerry ended up staying on board for a significant period of time. Our open and healthy dialogue during negotiations was a great experience for us, and it worked well for all parties involved.

How to Make Vital Secret #20 Work for You

There are five things you need to do in order to be gracious and smile when you leave. You'll need to leave when the time is right, don't brag about the price you got them to pay, don't criticize the buyer, leave a little sooner than expected, and take a break.

1. Leave when the time is right.

When it comes time to leave, don't hang around. Doing so makes it awkward for everyone—old employees, the new owner, and you. The time is right when you are no longer happy with what you do. When the time comes, leave as quickly as possible without negatively impacting the business.

2. Don't brag about the price you got them to pay.

Although your ego will want to boast about your success, no one will appreciate it, especially the buyer of your business. So under no circumstance should you boast about the amount you received. Try to be discrete. Don't disclose numbers when you're discussing the sale, because at the end of the day, it will only make the buyers angry, and you may end up with a reputation for taking advantage of people.

3. Don't criticize the buyer.

It's also important that after the acquisition occurs, you be complimentary about the acquirer. This holds true whether you become an employee of the new business, you leave, or things end on a sour note. There is no advantage in being condescending toward the way the buyer is running your former company.

In many instances, you'll be tempted to say why the business is nowhere near as good as when you were CEO. I heard this repeatedly from entrepreneurs I interviewed. They all saw the mistakes the sellers made, but they didn't discuss these things with anyone, including their former employees.

When I would receive calls from former employees talking about the way the company was being run, I would remind them that GE had been very successful in the past and that there was a reason behind the way they were doing things. My guess was that GE Financial was going to do a whole lot more with my old company than I ever could have. This was seldom the answer my former employees wanted, but it was the reality of the situation and there was no benefit to speaking negatively.

The decisions your buyer makes may be right, or they may be wrong. Still, it makes no difference whatsoever. It's their company to do with it what they will. Remember the story of Nakia. You won't know the company's fortune or the impact of the decisions they're making until time passes. So prepare yourself to wish the company and your former employees well.

4. Leave a little sooner than expected.

Regardless of why you're leaving, it'll help you, the acquirer, and your former employees, if you leave on your own terms. It is in everyone's best interest that you leave a favorable impression as you head out the door, and this means not being forced out by the buyer. Doing so may cause your old employees to resent the buyer.

5. Take a break.

Enjoy your victory, and then find something else to do. Most importantly, take your time. This is advice I wish I would have listened to. Everyone told me to take some time to relax and decompress. Despite my own worries when we sold Centurion, you should take that advice. Your brain will not rot, you will not lose your ability to think, and your contacts will not disappear. You need to relax, even if it takes months or years. Adjust to your new reality, and then find something to do. No matter how much money you have, if you don't continue to grow, it'll be easy for you to stagnate.

I'd like to finish with a story that I think is fitting for the end of the book. Recently, I went to Mongolia with some other successful entrepreneurs. We were flying on the private jet of a man named Robert, someone who has made well over a billion dollars building and selling companies. During our flight, I asked him why he continued working.

"Robert, I have to ask. Why are you still doing this? You clearly don't need the money, so why continue to work and fly all over the world to grow your companies?"

"Joe," he told me, "I have a great place in Thailand. In fact, I think it's the best place in the world to retire. When I'm there, it's a phenomenal place to be. I have a home on the beach, I get a massage every day, and I do nothing but relax. But you can only get so many massages and take so many walks on the beach before you feel the urge to do something. So I just do what I can do well, and that's build businesses. When I'm done, I go to Thailand and get my massages. But since I have to do something, why not do what I'm good at?"

■■■■

You'll go through a huge range of emotions as you go through the process of building and selling a company. Some of your biggest challenges will become your greatest victories, but leaving and turning your back on everything might be one of the toughest challenges you'll face. As you go, know that you have made a difference and created something of value in the world. This makes you braver than most, and you should feel confident that it was not a coincidence. Your success wasn't just luck. You had to be there to make it happen, and you can be there again if you so choose.

Head into a new chapter of your life with the same passion with which you lived your old one. Remember the story of Nakia; don't second-guess yourself, because you'll never know how fortunate you are until you are able to look back on your decisions.

You'll never know the true nature of your fortune until it has passed.

Congratulations on having the courage to try what so few attempt—to make an impact and change the world in some small way. Good luck and may you achieve all the success you desire.

Index